D1153853

MEGAN KARR

TATE PUBLISHING
AND ENTERPRISES, LLC

Published by Tate Publishing & Enterprises, LLC
127 E. Trade Center Terrace | Mustang, Oklahoma 73064 USA
1.888.361.9473 | www.tatepublishing.com

Tate Publishing is committed to excellence in the publishing industry. The company reflects the philosophy established by the founders, based on Psalm 68:11,
"The Lord gave the word and great was the company of those who published it."

Book design copyright © 2015 by Tate Publishing, LLC. All rights reserved.
Cover design by Niño Carlo Suico
Interior design by Mary Jean Archival

Published in the United States of America

ISBN: 978-1-68118-924-6
Historical Fiction
15.04.21

To the one who saved me

Preface

I loved her, but he swept her off her feet—something I wish I could have done years ago. I never had the nerve. I eventually told her, but she had the baby to think about.

I tried to warn her, but she was too stubborn. They were happy once, but he destroyed her, like I knew he would. I tried to get her to turn back, but she would not listen to a word of it, at least not at first. What is it like to watch the one person you would die for crumble under the pressure of love and loss? Well, I hope you never find out.

My love, my life, my best friend. She came back to me, and there I stood as scared as death. I had to take my chance before it was too late, before she moved past me without even looking back as if to whisper a faint "I love you."

No more whispering, not today.

You see, love is a strange thing: you can go all your life searching for it, but never really understand what it is until it is staring you in the face. Then, once it's gone, it's gone, and no one has yet to figure out how to get it back. The thing with love is that you can't be afraid to take it when it comes, because you never know when it will come again or how long it will last. Well, my love for her will never fade, and that is something worth writing about. She is something worth writing about.

Chapter 1

New Orleans 1925

Isabella Archer made her way down the lively streets of New Orleans with youth in her heart and a swing in her step. She wore a loose-fitting green dress with fringe down the front. Her black gloves graced her delicate hands and her natural red smile lined her white teeth. She looked to her left and saw her childhood friends, Irene Matthews and Irene's older brother, Lucas. Isabella walked toward them through the crowded street and commented on Irene's black dress and feather. The cobblestone under her feet was unstable, so she took Lucas's free arm to steady her weight. She smiled at him with her chocolate eyes, and he laughed at her with his friendly green ones. Isabella glanced up at Lucas and commented, "I see you dolled up for this occasion, Lucas."

He gave her a quick smile and then elbowed his sister. "You know I spend hours getting ready for outings such as these."

"Oh, hush, brother. No one wants to hear you beat your gums," Irene said with a distinct playfulness in her hazel eyes.

Isabella blushed on Lucas's behalf. "I don't suppose your brother revels in spending his nights with us dames."

"I rather enjoy it actually," he said with a boyish grin. Isabella noticed small lines on his forehead and came to realize that the small boy she once knew had aged. Isabella felt her own skin and was relieved it was still tight. Being twenty-seven, Isabella knew her time to age was coming soon, but she was not as fixated on it as Irene. Irene used creams and herbs to keep her youth, even though she was only one year Isabella's senior.

The friends passed an unstable man who seemed to have illegal liquor in a brown bag. Isabella was disgusted that a man would drink to the point that he could no longer stand. The streets smelled of vomit and urine, thanks to men who loved their bourbon more than their lives. She scrunched her nose, and Lucas commented, "Charming isn't it?"

She rolled her eyes and Irene let out a loud laugh. They walked up to the party as smooth jazz music filled the moist air. The sound of the saxophone was carried by the wind, and it enchanted Isabella from the moment it touched her ears. They walked into the joint and saw many people dancing to the revolutionary music. Isabella engaged in some static conversation but was quickly unimpressed and ready to leave;

nonetheless, Irene encouraged her to stay a while and enjoy the music. Lucas excused himself to talk with a buddy from the university. Isabella looked around the room to find other familiar faces, but her eyes followed Lucas. He was thirty years old, but looked as if he was still in his twenties. He was a reputable man and a great brother to Irene. Isabella smiled as she thought of their previous years together. Isabella looked to her right and saw that Irene was no longer there. She searched the room for her and saw her dancing with a decent-looking man. Isabella smiled at her friend and enjoyed the music for which Irene begged her to stay.

Weary from the walk, Isabella found a seat in the corner of the room and sat down to take in the sights and sounds. She finished her tea and licked her lips, satisfied that she was no longer thirsty. She looked around the room for her friends and saw that they were having a wonderful time. Lucas was chatting with a friend, and Irene was dancing the night away. Isabella had never been one for crowds. She closed her eyes and listened to the soft melodic jazz but turned when she felt a man staring at her. His eyes were like needles up her spine. He wore a dark gray suit, a maroon tie, and held a hat in his hand. His jawline was perfectly defined and his brown hair fell across his forehead. He smiled at her. Isabella felt her heart race as she gave him a polite smile. He gestured to the seat next to her and politely asked, "May I take a seat here, miss?"

She looked at his friendly smile and replied, "I suppose it wouldn't hurt."

He took a seat and the two sat silently for a while. Isabella decided to focus on the music and not the stranger to her left. He was attractive and did not look to be a schemer or bootlegger. Yet there was something mysterious about him. In all her time in New Orleans, she had never seen him. Isabella laughed at herself for thinking this, because New Orleans was a large city, and there was no possible way she knew everyone who had ever entered it. She could tell the man heard her small giggle, and her cheeks grew red. He moved closer to her and asked, "May I ask what you are laughing at?"

"Myself, I'm afraid," she said with a small grin on her red lips. Isabella turned back to listen to the music, but she felt his eyes on her and turned to ask, "What's your name?"

"I thought you'd never ask. My name is Raymond Dailey. What's yours?"

Isabella was enchanted. She fixed a small piece of hair on her head and replied, "Isabella Archer. What brings you here?"

"Some old friends from my school days. I'm sure you know some of them."

"You're so sure, but you've never met me," she said with a roll of her eyes.

Raymond laughed and replied, "I only guess, because this is a reunion celebration after all."

Isabella snapped her head and put her hand to her chest as if she had no idea that the party was for Lucas's graduation reunion. She gasped melodramatically and flirted, "I had no idea that this was a closed party. How foolish of me!"

She saw Raymond's eyes brighten as dimples formed on his cheeks. "You're a very bold woman, Isabella Archer."

"I hope that's not a problem for you, Raymond Dailey."

"I rather like a woman who's bold enough to speak her mind," he said as he sat closer to her.

Isabella felt her stomach flutter as if there were butterflies inside. "Who did you come with?" she asked as she tucked a black curl behind her head.

"I came with myself. The question is, who did you come with? I assume you're not always a cancelled stamp like you are tonight."

Isabella pointed to Lucas and replied, "I'm here with Lucas Matthews and his sister. Do you know him?"

Raymond tilted his head as he studied Lucas. He shrugged his shoulders and answered, "I suppose we were friends once, but I don't remember him well."

Isabella watched Lucas dance with Irene and smiled. She could sense that Raymond believed she and Lucas were going together, so she commented, "We've been friends since childhood."

"Nothing more?"

"There was something more once, but that was long ago."

Isabella turned to see Raymond's eyebrow lift. He put his arm around her and looked into her eyes. She internally pleaded for Lucas to come over and ruin the moment, but at the same time, she did not want the moment to end. Isabella looked down and Raymond kissed her cheek. Isabella was shocked by his kiss and retreated. She saw that he was offended by her action and commented, "I was not expecting that."

"Neither was I," he said with a dashing grin. "I'd like to see you again, Isabella."

"I would like that too."

"Very well."

Isabella shook her head, and Raymond took her hand. Feeling a bit warm, Isabella looked up to watch Lucas and Irene but found that Lucas was already looking at her. The look on his face was one she had never seen before. It was a look of despair and hatred mixed with joy and sorrow, and when their eyes met, Isabella felt a jolt of energy. She saw Lucas put down his drink and walk over to them, and within ten seconds, Lucas was standing before them both.

Lucas looked at Isabella and his heart sunk. He looked at Raymond Dailey and felt sick to his stomach, but mustered up a smile and commented, "I see you've met Mr. Dailey."

"I thought you didn't know Lucas."

"I do remember him now. It seems age has messed with my mind," Raymond said with an annoying grin on his selfish lips. Lucas knew Raymond's reputation and was appalled that Isabella would even think of speaking to such a man. Lucas took Isabella's hand and swallowed as he looked into Raymond's eyes. "I believe it's time me and my friends get going."

"We've just arrived, Lucas," Isabella commented, looking at him and then to Raymond.

"I believe it best we go, Isabella," Lucas said with a tight chest.

Lucas had never liked Raymond Dailey, and he certainly did not like him now. He had the mind to tell Mr. Dailey to dry up and beat it or he would rough him up for good; a reunion was not a proper place for such things, Lucas knew. There was an odd feeling Lucas got when he was around Raymond that could not be explained. All the more, he did not want Isabella hanging around a potato like Raymond Dailey. He felt Irene behind him and told her it was time to go.

Before he left, Lucas looked into Raymond's cobra-like eyes and tried to send a warning that he would shelter Isabella from him at all costs. Although, it was clear that Raymond would not heed the warning. The women left before Lucas, but he was behind them on the way home, watching the many intoxicated men on the street. He knew that Isabella would be upset with him for cutting off her conversation with Raymond, but it was for the best. She was such a wonderful woman with much potential and a caring heart. Lucas did not want to see her wasted on a fool like Raymond because she was worth much more than that.

"Why were you so upset back there? I was only making friends," Isabella said.

"I don't like him," Lucas explained as they reached her home.

"Just because you two are not best buddies doesn't mean that I can't be friends with him," Isabella said, frustrated with Lucas's childlike behavior.

Lucas turned to Isabella and replied sternly, "I just want you to be careful, Isabella."

"I'm a grown woman, Lucas…"

"You know I don't want to see you hurt, right?" he interrupted as if he was apologizing for stating his opinion.

"I know," Isabella replied.

"Don't do something or befriend someone who could harm you."

Isabella looked into her friend's caring eyes and wished he would confess his buried feelings. He wouldn't. She hugged Lucas and replied, "I can take care of myself, Lucas."

Chapter 2

The next afternoon, Isabella went to fetch the mail and saw a letter from Raymond. How he found her address, she did not care. "I'll pick you up for dinner, Ms. Archer." The letter was short and to the point, something Isabella was fond of: why waste words if they are said with no meaning? As a teacher, she always told her students that too many words are like too much traffic, useless and frustrating. Isabella smiled when she heard Lucas's voice in her head, *Words are the fruit and our lives are the trees. We need both.* It was a horrible metaphor, but it had always made her laugh. The clock struck four, and Isabella hurried home to get ready for Raymond's call. She had never been more excited to see a man than her first date with Lucas, but that was over five years ago. Isabella rolled her eyes and pushed the thought of Lucas out of her head—the past was the past.

Isabella powdered her face carefully and applied her lipstick. She put on her favorite casual dress and a long-beaded necklace. Her heart jumped when she heard a knock on her front door. She checked her face in the mirror one last time before leaving her room to let Raymond in. When she opened the door, she saw him dressed in a casual suit. "How do you do?"

"Well, and you?"

"Splendid!" Raymond replied as he offered her his arm. "Ready?"

"Yes," she replied as she quickly grabbed her purse.

Isabella and Raymond walked into a small restaurant where the waiters knew Raymond by name. Isabella took off her scarf and her beads fell into place around her neck. She looked over the menu but glanced up to see Raymond looking at her with a charming smile. Isabella laughed but covered her face with the menu, hoping Raymond would not see her blush. His suit was different than the last he wore, but similar in style. Isabella put her napkin in her lap and felt the sequins on her dress. Raymond ordered first, and she followed his lead, careful not to get anything priced above his dish. The napkins were a beautiful purple and the water glasses were lined with gold at the top. Isabella smiled at him as he leaned on the table. "What do you like to do, Isabella?" he asked.

She finished a sip of the refreshing ice water and replied, "I like to read."

His brow folded in and he gave a smirk. "A woman who likes to read."

"It's not uncommon, you know," she said with a blank look on her face.

He stared at her intently and nerves sprung up in her chest. He took a breath and laughed, "I'm only joking."

She brushed her fingers through her hair, thankful that he was only joking with her. Isabella had a good feeling that she would be stuck on this man for a good while. All her life, no man, besides Lucas, had ever paid attention to her. Her father was kind but never present, something Lucas always succeeded in. The night went on very well and Raymond was as charming as ever. "How do you like your food?"

"It's delicious," she replied between small bites.

Raymond stuffed bread in his mouth and chewed before replying, "You're a teacher?"

"Yes. And you?"

"I'm a businessman. Various things."

"What kind of things?"

"Mostly money. I deal with some large businesses and keep track of their income and output."

"Interesting."

"Do you have any siblings?"

Isabella sipped her water. "No."

"Parents?"

"No."

"Oh."

"Do you have siblings or parents?"

"I have two brothers and a sister. My parents live in New York."

"I'd love to have siblings. What are yours like?"

"My brothers Matthew and David live in Boston, and my sister Myrtle lives in New York with her husband, George."

"How lovely!"

"I suppose," he said with a small smile.

"Lucas and Irene are the only kind of family I have."

"I see. I'm glad for you."

They continued to eat until they were satisfied. Isabella was happy the night ended after supper, because she was still getting used to the idea of falling for someone other than Lucas.

They pulled into the drive at nine o'clock, and he helped her out of the car. Raymond looked at her with his welcoming light brown eyes, and her heart fluttered. She smiled and thanked him for the meal, but he insisted on walking her to her door. Isabella looked back at Raymond and commented, "You know, I believe you were my first real date."

"Was I really?" he asked in a sincerely shocked voice. "What about Lucas?"

"Doesn't count!" she said with more force than what was necessary.

"I would've thought every guy in town would want to be with you, Isabella Archer."

She rolled her eyes and replied, "Well, I'm afraid most guys think I'm nothing more than a flat tire."

"You're more than they say you are, Isabella," Raymond said as he came closer to her, "I'd like to see you again, if you'll have me."

Her stomach felt like mush, and she did not know whether to cry or vomit. Isabella looked at her feet and then into the face of the man before her, "I'd like that, Raymond."

He gave a dashing smile. Raymond nodded his head in a bashful manner as he backed off the front porch. He got into his car and left her home for his. When she was finally alone, her mind began to race; how could a man like Raymond Dailey be interested in a woman like her? She was nothing but a teacher who lived in her late parents' home, hoping one day to marry a man, a man like Raymond. Isabella unlocked her front door and walked into the dark home. She grabbed some extra cash, knowing she had to visit Irene before the night was over.

Irene washed the plates in the small kitchen as Lucas straightened the small living area that contained one old couch and two rocking chairs, both made by their grandfather. Lucas took the trash and put it in the bin by the sink. He looked at his sister and offered, "I'll do them so you can rest."

She gave him a grand smile and thanked her big brother for his help, and again for the roof over her head. Since their parents died, Lucas and Irene had been on their own. Lucas was successful enough to live in the city, and Irene was one of the most desired ladies in town. Lucas took off his coat, tie, dress shoes, and vest as he rolled up his sleeves to work. The food came off the dishes well, except for the pan, which needed extra scrubbing. As he placed the pan in the water to soak, he heard a loud slam of their front door and a voice saying, "I think I'm stuck for good, Irene!"

From the moment the first word trickled out of her mouth, Lucas could tell that the voice was Isabella's. He shook his head and continued to work on the pan, all the while listening to the conversation in the room behind him.

Isabella glanced at the faded wallpaper that covered the wall behind Irene as she waited for a reply. Isabella looked at her friend's confused expression and explained further. "I went on a date with Raymond tonight."

Irene looked at her with a small, but noticeable, frown and began to ask Isabella why she went with Raymond to begin with. Isabella could give no answer but that he seemed nice; Irene's expression warned her to think carefully about what was said next. After thinking a short while, she came out with, "I think I could marry a man like him."

Irene shook her head, her blond curls bouncing. "You barely know him, Isabella."

"That doesn't matter if it's love," she replied with a bitter tone. Isabella sat by Irene and asked, "Do you not trust me?"

Irene batted her eyes. "I don't trust him."

"You don't know him, Irene," Isabella argued, raising her voice.

"Neither do you," a voice commented from behind.

Isabella turned around to see Lucas; someone who she had forgotten resided in the same apartment as Irene. Her face blushed for an unknown reason, but possibly because she knew she was wrong and he was right. The two friends looked at each other for a moment until Lucas joined them in the living room. Isabella waited for Lucas to give her a lecture on how to behave, but was shocked to hear him ask, "Why do you love him?"

He rested his elbows on his knees and his head on his hands, but Isabella knew that inside he was dying to scold her. She looked to Irene and then to Lucas. Irene gave a shrug and motioned for her to answer the question that was suffocating the three of them. Isabella gave a simple shrug and replied, "He treats me well."

Lucas rolled his eyes, and Isabella knew a sermon was about to spew out of his mouth. He lifted his head and asked, "Is that all?"

Isabella was stunned again and rubbed her hands on her sequined gown. She looked at Irene, who was fixed on her brother, and asked, "What do you think, Irene?"

Isabella watched as Irene cleared her throat and folded her hands to say, "I agree with Lucas. The choice is yours, you can love him or not."

"Is that it then?" Isabella asked, looking for a smile from either one of her friends. "I thought you would be happy for me."

Lucas stood with a sigh and rubbed his eyes. "I don't like him, Isabella, you know that. I don't condone your relationship."

Fury raged through Isabella as she felt heat in the pit of her stomach. "Who are you to condone anything I do, Lucas?

You're my friend, not my chaperone or my father, and you're certainly not in a position to give me romantic advice."

Isabella watched as Lucas turned to face her with wide and violent eyes. It was then when Isabella immediately wished she could take back every word she had said.

Lucas's heart stopped for a moment as he looked at Isabella with the weight of silence surrounding them. He looked at her soft brown eyes and wished that he did not love her so much that he hated every inch of her in that moment. Lucas took a breath and breathed out with a huff. Seeing just how sorry Isabella was, he looked at her almost-perfect complexion and bit back a smile. "I didn't presume I was any of those things, Isabella. I just want what's best for you."

He could see the sorrow in her eyes when she asked him to forget what she said, but he couldn't. He loved her too much to forget anything she said. Lucas shook his head and focused on his anger with her to prevent himself from cracking a frustrated smile. "I think it would be best if you left."

Isabella blinked back evident tears and said good-bye to Irene, who walked her to the door, making sure she had a way home. Lucas, on the other hand, sat down and laughed as he ran his hands though his hair, frustrated that he cared so much. Isabella was his dearest friend, and he could not see her hurt, but she was too stubborn a match for even him. Isabella, he knew, would have to figure things out the hard way.

Chapter 3

Lucas placed his hands in the pockets of his pants and hung his head as he dragged himself to work. Upset by his disagreement with Isabella, Lucas was in no mood to write. He looked up from the street, hoping to see a friendly face. He then saw the face he detested most of all. He took a look at Raymond Dailey and clenched his fists, trying to hold back his anger. It was not that he had any significant proof that Mr. Dailey was a double-crosser, it was an innate sense. Nonetheless, however good Raymond's intensions were, they could still not cover up the stench of his evil aroma. Raymond seemed happy, which bothered Lucas even more. He stopped to wave at Lucas, which was surprising for a man like Raymond. Lucas smiled politely, but when Raymond commented about his previous date with Isabella, Lucas could no longer keep his emotions at bay. He looked at Raymond and stated with a calm tone, "Don't hurt her, Raymond."

"I'd never harm a woman," Raymond said with a small smirk.

"Isabella's a fine woman, Raymond, and if you hurt her in anyway I swear you'll regret it," Lucas warned as he tightened his eyes and his grip.

Raymond pulled away from the handshake, and Lucas could see an ever-present evil camouflaged in his charming smile. "I won't hurt her, my friend."

The men parted ways, but Lucas watched as Raymond rounded the corner to Isabella's home. He was sickened by the thought of Isabella and Raymond and decided he needed to turn his thoughts in a different direction. He looked both ways as he crossed the street and headed toward his work, hoping that the monotony of the day would drown out his fears for Isabella.

Isabella awoke to birds outside her window singing as if it was their occupation to usher in the morning sun. She felt like she was waking from a dream that had not ended. She was stuck on Raymond, and she knew he felt the same for her. It hurt that Lucas did not approve, but she could not think of Lucas Matthews anymore. She and Raymond were perfect for each other. His boldness compensated for her shyness, and his utter disregard for emotion balanced out her overemotional self. She looked in her mirror and dressed for the day. Isabella slid on a low-waist green dress and a pair of short heels. She sat a fashionable hat on her black hair and gave herself a smile. She powdered her nose as she heard a knock at her front door.

Isabella opened her red door and let Raymond into her home. He was dressed nicely, as usual, which gave her the heebie-jeebies. She looked at Raymond and knew that she was going goofy for him. It had to be love; if it was not then what else could it be? It was almost like she and Raymond were pulled together by fate and instructed to live out life together. She took Raymond's strong arm, and the two began their day together.

"Long time no see," Raymond said with a coy smile.

"Hello, dear."

"I just ran into Lucas. He seemed upset."

Isabella rolled her eyes and replied, "Never mind him. We had a disagreement last night, and I bet he's still upset."

"He just wants to protect you."

"I know. He means well," Isabella said as they rounded the corner to eat breakfast in the same restaurant.

"He seemed tense this morning."

"Please, Raymond, let's not talk about Lucas. Please?"

Raymond nodded as he opened the door for her, like a true gentleman.

It was not until later that day that Lucas put his feet on the couch to relax for the night. He brushed his hands through his brown hair and rubbed his temples. The day had not been one of his brightest, but he hoped that he would see Isabella at their usual Friday-night gathering so he could apologize to her. Irene entered the room with a smirk on her cherry-red lips. She sat by Lucas and, as her brother, he could tell that her day had been the opposite of his. Lucas looked at Irene and asked, "What is it?"

"Lucas, you'll never guess who I saw today," she said with an incandescent glow.

He shrugged his shoulders and watched his sister's eyes come to life. "Fred Hartley from grade school."

"Fredrick Hartley, that's baloney, Fred moved to New York."

"Apparently he moved back down here for work and to be close to family," she said as her cheeks turned a rosy pink.

Lucas looked at his sister's girlish smile and laughed. "You can't still be stuck on Fred, can you?"

Irene opened her mouth as if Lucas had offended her by even knowing she had feelings for any of his friends. Lucas smiled when she retorted, "That's none of your beeswax!"

"I bet you think he's the bee's knees, Irene," he teased. "I know you always have, and just to let you know, he thought the world of you then as well."

Irene's petite face lit up at the news. "We were children then, Lucas and I were only twelve when I started going soft."

Lucas looked at his sister's blue dress and matching hat, which happened to be her favorite outfit. Ashamed he knew his sister's favorite dress, he commented, "I'm not a fool, Irene. He was my best friend. I know he kissed you."

Irene's face melted into an embarrassed expression as she gave him a cold stare that cut through his temporary jovial state. She blinked, "He told you?"

Lucas sat up and put his hands together as he replied, "He was my best guy, Irene, and we told each other everything." He took his sister's hands, "I know he still carries a torch for you, and he'd marry you anytime, anyplace."

Irene smiled and replied, "I wrote him, you know."

Lucas's eyes widened as he replied, "No, did he write back?"

"Every time. I suppose we've been friends all these years he's been away. It was only four years, but it seemed like forever."

Lucas saw his sister's eyes light up at the thought of marriage to Fred. Lucas squeezed his sister's hand, hoping that she knew that he would more than bless their marriage. To think that his best friend would soon be his brother was a pleasant thought. Lucas knew Fred well enough to know that his coming to town had nothing to do with a job or family, but everything to do with Irene. He decided to keep that to himself, because he was sure Irene would soon find that out on her own.

Isabella tossed a piece of bread to the small duck across from her and Irene's bench. She was happy that their Friday nights were spent with each other, no matter how mad she was at Lucas. The night was beautiful, and the streets of New Orleans were alive. Isabella looked at the birds, but gave the leftover bread to Lucas, who promptly turned away from her. Isabella rolled her eyes, and a small heated laugh escaped from her mouth. She looked at Lucas, who was looking at a wall, and felt sorry for the words she said to him the previous day. However, she had a right to be angry with him. Irene tapped her shoulder, which momentarily frightened her. Isabella looked at her shaking friend and asked, "What is it, Irene?"

"I'm so nervous. I haven't spent very much time with Fred these past years."

Isabella felt for her friend, but knew that Irene was too focused on what could go wrong. She had always been that way. Isabella looked at Irene and fixed a stray blond hair that had escaped from under her hat. "Baloney. You know Fred Hartley better than he knows himself, and you have thousands of letters to prove it."

Isabella could see Irene's features soften after hearing those words. Isabella's own self-esteem rose when she saw Irene's glowing face. It was nice to be speaking to at least one of her close friends. Irene was wearing her blue dress and matching hat, which was quite flattering. It brought out her mature features and kind eyes. Irene was fidgeting with her dress. "Why are you so nervous?"

Irene looked at Lucas and then back to Isabella. "My brother told me he believes Fred will marry me."

"And how! Fred should marry you, Irene."

Irene's attention was quickly snatched when Fred entered the street from outside his place of work. He was a good-looking man, no doubt. He had black hair, hazel eyes, and a stylish mustache that lined the top of his lip. Irene took a breath and walked across the street to him. They embraced, and Isabella's heart warmed at the sight of her friend's lighthearted expression of affection.

Fred Hartley and Irene Matthews were a couple that seemed to fit perfectly together. His charm, and her sense molded to form one beautiful picture of happy love and ultimate matrimony. Isabella thought of Raymond, and how she planned their match being her first and final, like Irene's.

Fred and Irene crossed the street to meet Isabella. She greeted them with a friendly smile saying, "I'm glad that you two are happy."

"Very much so, Isabella. It's nice to see you again," Fred said taking his eyes off Irene for the first time that night.

Isabella felt someone behind her. She looked up and saw Lucas's face, but kept her eyes forward as she continued to smile, hoping that the night would not be too long.

Lucas took a breath and prayed that his actions would not be as disgraceful as they were the previous night. He looked down at Isabella and his heart jumped, but he smiled at his old friend and commented, "You look quite spiffy tonight, Fred."

He watched as Fred's eyes lit up. "I never thought I'd see you and Isabella together again, Lucas."

Lucas felt his stomach drop as he stared forward. He tried to speak with his frantic and wild eyes, but Fred was too blind to see it. He cleared his throat, not knowing what to say.

Isabella replied, "We're only friends. As a matter of fact, I'm with Raymond Dailey."

Fred looked at Lucas as if to suggest that Lucas still felt things other than friendship for Isabella, which Lucas certainly did not want to be public knowledge. He and Fred were friends in school and as young men they talked of girls they would one day like to marry. Fred always knew he would marry Irene, but Lucas had suspicions that the woman he desired to be his wife would be taken from him. Lucas laughed at the irony of the present day where both things were about to occur. Lucas rolled his eyes, and Fred patted his back with clear understanding as they all made their way to see a new film.

Chapter 4

November was Lucas's favorite month, but as this month ended and Christmas rolled around, Lucas still worried for Isabella. He, Fred, and Raymond were the last of his friends to be single, but Lucas had a feeling that would soon change. Fred and Irene had spent everyday together since he returned, which was a fantastic development. However, as he watched Isabella grow more and more attached to Raymond, the more he desired to wipe Raymond from the planet for good. He tucked in his shirt and buttoned his vest, still numb to the fact that another Christmas had come. He called Irene into the room to help him with his tie. She was wearing a light pink gown with silver stitching and beading. Her dark gloves went past her elbows, and her black hat sat on her blond head, and her white pearls hung around her neck. "You'd look like a flapper if you had shorter hair."

"I'm ignoring you, Lucas. It's the newest style. Things are changing."

"Things have already changed," he said in a melodramatic tone.

Lucas watched his sister's playful smile harden into a non-responsive scowl. "Isabella can make her own mistakes, and you need to make a few of your own."

Lucas sat on the couch and asked, "What does that mean?"

His sister sat with him and took his hand, "You're so much better than her, Lucas. I love her, but I love you too. You have so much to offer the world."

"So does she."

Lucas watched as Irene pressed her lips together and asked, "You moved on years ago, so why is this bothering you now?"

"He's a bad man, Irene," Lucas replied as he shook his head with regret.

"Trust that Isabella will make the right choice," Irene encouraged as she motioned for Lucas to follow her.

He stood up and confessed, "I just feel like it's my job to save her."

"But it's not, is it?"

Lucas took a breath and thanked God for his wise sister, who always reminded him to fully trust in the one who loves him the most.

Lucas walked out of the apartment and toward the annual Christmas party he knew Isabella and Raymond were going to attend. Irene took his arm and commented, "Fred's coming, and you're welcome to stay by us for the night if Raymond gets to you."

Lucas thanked his sister for her kind offer, but thought it would be best to face his problems head-on. After all, Isabella was an intelligent woman, who would never choose a man like Raymond in the end.

Isabella ran her hands down her black low-waist dress and took Raymond's arm. She looked into his promising eyes and could not help but notice his strange behavior. She knew that something was wrong with him, but she could not tell what he was thinking. Isabella looked forward and met eyes with Lucas as she passed him. She saw his eyes glaze over and wondered if she was making the right choice in staying with Raymond, even when her closest friend detested the match. He had a keen eye for personalities; she knew that. So why had she not taken his advice and never even entertained the idea of Raymond Dailey? She looked at Raymond's profile, and his confidence outshone any flaw he could possibly have. Isabella felt as if she was making the right choice, because Raymond obviously loved her, which was more than any other man had done for her in her life. Maybe Lucas was just jealous that she was the first to truly move on.

As the night went on, she could sense Raymond getting stranger and stranger. She scanned the room for faces she knew and saw Irene and Fred talking together in a corner of the room. Her heart warmed at the sight, and she was happy for her friend. She knew that Irene had waited many years to finally be with Fred. Isabella remembered the tears that came after his departure those four years ago, but as she looked at them now, she envied every ounce of pain Irene felt. Would she and Raymond share that kind of passion? Would Raymond leave New Orleans, a town he loved, for her? Even though Irene had no knowledge of it, it was clear that she was the reason Fred left New York.

Isabella looked at Lucas, who seemed to be watching her, and wondered what life would be like with him. Just as her thoughts turned to Lucas, Raymond tapped her on the shoulder and took her hand. With no time to think, she was up on the stage with Raymond and the jazz band. As they finished their energetic song, they fell silent. All Isabella could hear was the sound of her beating heart. She had never been one for crowds, and she had a feeling of what was going to happen next. Isabella watched as Raymond took a knee in front of her. Her stomach dropped. Isabella closed her eyes and focused on her breathing as Raymond asked, "Isabella Archer, my friend, my dream, my love, will you do me the honor and marry me?"

Isabella was frozen as she looked into the eyes of the man she thought she loved, but felt Lucas's warning eye on her. Was a life of happiness worth the risk of losing a friend like Lucas and the support of a friend like Irene? Happiness was in front of her, she had been proposed to, an offer that would most likely never come again. She took Raymond's hands and helped him up as she softly replied, "Yes."

Lucas dropped his glass as the crowd around him cheered for the happy couple. He watched as Raymond put his hands around Isabella and kissed her lips. She kissed him back and with every kiss Lucas grew more and more uncomfortable. He took a breath to hold back his anger as he walked out of the mansion and into the adjacent garden. The night was cool, but he did not mind the cold. He took the rocks that laid at his feet and began to throw them at the walls of Raymond's father's large home. Lucas's chest ached, and his breath was hard to catch as he chunked rocks at the future of which he once dreamed. He could not keep his eyes from pouring out the tears he had held in for what seemed like a hundred years. Lucas needed to feel the pain of Isabella's loss. If he didn't, it would be as if she was never gone. Lucas lost track of time as he stood there in his grief and anger. There was a small whimper of a voice behind him. He looked back to see his sister standing behind him. He saw a soft look of sorrow in her understanding eyes. He swallowed and wiped his face with his sleeve, getting rid of any evidence that he had been crying. Lucas cleared his throat and commented, "There's nothing to see here."

He stood still as Irene approached him slowly, timid that she might see through his hardened facade. He watched her fold her arms across her stomach as she inquired, "What's eating you?"

He rolled his eyes and let out a sigh. "Just taking a walk to clear my head."

"She left with him an hour ago, Lucas," Irene said with the tenderness only a sister could share.

Lucas let out a sarcastic laugh. "Why did *he* leave? This is his father's house."

He rubbed his forehead as Irene came closer to him with widening eyes. It was then that she realized Lucas's secret. "You never did get over her, did you?"

He gave a small bittersweet smile as he raised his sweaty brow, "I love her. I've always loved her, and I always will."

Irene shook her head. "Lucas, she's getting married. There comes a time when we all have to move on."

He began to raise his voice saying, "There's no moving on, Irene. I love her and that poison will cripple me until the day I die."

"She had no part in any of it, Lucas," Irene defended.

Lucas was so infuriated with himself that he threw a rock at the wall. He turned to his sister, calmly stating through his teeth, "She had everything to do with it, and you know it. She chose him. Am I not the clear choice? Have I not done everything, right?"

"You lost her just as I lost Fred."

"Fred returned, Irene. Fred's here now, and I'm sure he came back to New Orleans for you, but you're just too blind to see it. He never stopped loving you, and he never will, just as I have never stopped loving Isabella. There's no use in moving on, you see, because we're nowhere to begin with."

"That's your fault, not hers," Irene said as she stepped toward her brother.

Tears filled Lucas's eyes, and he shook his head, slowly taking a seat on the ground. The pounding in his forehead increased, and he knew that it was he who had made the biggest mistake of all. He looked up at his sister and commented, "I did this."

Irene sat with her brother and replied, "You have to forget her, Lucas."

He looked in his sister's comforting eyes and confessed, "That's just it, I can't."

Chapter 5

Two days later, Isabella knocked on the Matthews' door with a bold grin on her painted lips. Irene opened the door and invited her into her and Lucas's small apartment. The walls were still a familiar green color, and the scent of perfume and smoke welcomed her into the room. She turned to her right to see Lucas sitting at a table smoking as he read the morning paper. This sight was puzzling to Isabella, because as far as she knew, Lucas was not a smoker, despite the popularity of it. She smiled as she walked up to her friend and commented, "You know, a friend once told me that smoking was no good."

Lucas looked up from the paper and gave her a disappointed look. He returned to reading, not saying a word, which took Isabella by surprise. Lucas had always laughed at her jokes, especially when they were about him. She looked at the bags under his eyes and asked, "What's eating you?"

Isabella saw the frustration in Lucas's eyes and felt sorrow overcome her. He looked at her again and then returned to his paper. She slid her hands on her green dress and stated, "Raymond and I are going to be married."

With a look up from his paper to her ring, Lucas commented, "You slay me."

Isabella frowned. She licked her lips as she took a deep breath, hoping Lucas would look up at her. She rolled her eyes and let out, "Says you."

She could see the betrayal hidden in Lucas's soft eyes as he replied, "You know, once upon a time I believed you had a decent head on your shoulders."

"Excuse me!" she exclaimed with an open mouth and wide chocolate eyes. Just in time, Irene rounded the corner as she fastened her earring to her ear. Isabella looked at Lucas, who still refused to look her in the eye.

Irene commented, "Let's go, Isabella."

Isabella looked at her friend reading the paper and felt pity for him. It was not her fault that Raymond asked her to marry him, and it was not her fault that Lucas didn't. Isabella was not blind, but she could not wait around forever either. She took a breath and looked at Irene and replied, "Let's get going, Raymond and I have plans tonight."

Lucas watched as his sister and her friend walked out of the room and into the streets of New Orleans. He closed the paper and took a breath as he choked back tears. Frustrated that Isabella would be so inconsiderate, he threw the paper against the wall and yelled out her name, as beautiful as it was. Lucas returned to his seat and pondered what was going on in Raymond's head. There was no way that Raymond Dailey would fall in love with a woman like Isabella Archer. She was much too intelligent for him. In fact, she was better than him in all areas of life, but he and Isabella refused to see it. Raymond had not proven to be a bad man, but something in Lucas told him to stay away from Raymond and to keep the people he loved away from him as well.

Irene rounded the corner of the street as a gust of vomit-scented wind hit her face. She looked to Isabella, who seemed to be as happy as ever, and sarcastically commented, "New Orleans, the greatest place in America."

Isabella gave a small smile, and Irene looked at her friend to see what was wrong. Isabella was a strong woman, and she had always looked on the brighter things in life. Irene looked at the people around her and came to realize how much society had changed in the past years since grade school. She still remembered going to school in a long dress, and goodness if her ankles showed. Now, women had cut their hair and dresses shorter. Fringe and sequins hung from her dress and from Isabella's. Irene turned to her friend. "So much has changed."

She watched as Isabella smiled and nodded, "Yes."

Irene looked at her beautiful, yet somehow broken, friend, and asked, "What is it, Isabella?"

Irene saw a tear in Isabella's eye as she replied, "What's love if my friends don't condone it?"

"Lucas has his own problems, Isabella. Anyways, I have something to tell you," Irene said with a smile and a fast-beating heart. Taking Isabella's hand. Irene gave a laugh as she exclaimed, "Fred has promised to propose to me!"

Isabella's eyes widened, and Irene could tell that she was happy for her. They embraced. "Good thing to know. I hope our weddings aren't going to be on the same day," Isabella replied with a smile.

Irene brushed her blond hair out of her face as she asked, "When are you planning to marry Raymond?"

Irene watched as Isabella's eyes lit up. "Three weeks from now." Her heart stood still when she heard her friend's words. Three weeks was not very long before marrying a man she just met. Not to mention, they had not known each other long before the engagement.

Isabella saw Irene's hesitant reaction and knew that she did not agree with the date. "Do you not approve?"

Isabella waited for an answer, but Irene stood there shaking her head. They continued to walk, but Isabella was no longer in the mood for a day with her friend. She turned to Irene and asked, "What's so wrong with Raymond?"

"It's all very fast," Irene replied as she crossed her hands over her chest.

"You and Fred are going to get engaged much faster than Raymond and me."

"We're not engaged yet, and even so, Fred and I have been friends all our lives, and you barely know Raymond," Irene explained.

Isabella grew angry, because after all this time her friends still did not trust her to make the right choices. She rolled her eyes and sneered, "I love him, Irene."

"I'm glad for you, but it's still a little fast."

Hurt by Irene's words, Isabella nodded and turned to go. She could hear Irene following her, so, Isabella turned around and said, "Leave me alone, Irene."

Irene left Isabella alone on the street to process what she said. Irene opened the door to her home and saw her brother lying on the couch with a glass in his hand. She shook her head, ashamed that Lucas would act so immature toward Isabella. Shaking him awake, Irene sat next to him and took his glass. "There's no good in this."

He looked at the glass and replied, "It was water, Irene."

Irene looked at the bags under her brother's eyes and recognized the smell that was coming from him. Not bathing was not suitable. She looked at her brother and hit him with the news, "Isabella's getting married in three weeks. There's nothing you can do."

She watched as her brother put his head in his hands and began to unleash the anger he had been keeping in since the proposal. He looked up to her with tired eyes and replied, "How am I supposed to hear it? How can I bear it, Irene?"

Placing her hand on his back, she replied, "You have to, Lucas. We both do."

"I don't like him, Irene. She has to know you don't like him either," he said with a look of determination Irene had never seen before.

"She knows. She's stubborn, Lucas. Isabella will have to learn the hard way."

"I'm afraid she won't learn in time."

Three weeks later, Isabella slipped into her white dress with the help of Irene, and tried to keep her tears from falling. She felt the fabric of her dress and knew that this day would be the best day of her life. She looked up to Irene and said, "I think I'm ready to go to my wedding."

Irene helped Isabella lift her dress and walk to the dressing area where she could see herself in a full-length mirror. Isabella touched her freshly curled hair, which was stiff, but beautiful, nonetheless. She looked at herself and felt as if she was in a dream. She touched her red-stained lips and her soft blushed cheeks as a small grin crept across her face. Isabella turned around and hugged her friend, thankful for someone who cared for her as a sister. Even if Lucas was against her marring Raymond, Isabella knew that Irene would stand by her until the end of time, like they promised years ago as children. Isabella opened her eyes wide and asked, "Well?"

"Aren't you a doll?" Irene asked with a chuckle in her voice.

Isabella playfully hit Irene with the fur wrap on her shoulder, and the two girls laughed together like they were ten years old. They walked out of the dressing room and into the hallway that connected to the church. Isabella looked at the lights above her and the red wallpaper on the wall to her right. She captured the moment in her mind, because she knew that this night would be a night she would want to remember for as long as she lived. The jazz band stopped playing, and the wedding march began. Isabella's stomach churned into knots. She put her hand to her stomach and looked at Irene with a white face. Irene's considerate eyes flickered as she commanded, "You look swell, now scram and marry the man you love."

Isabella nodded and took a breath as her friend exited through the church doors before her.

Lucas sat with a few of his friends from the university as he waited for the ceremony to begin. The flowers looked wilted, and his heart mirrored their downcast state. He closed his eyes and imagined what Isabella would look like. A smile slid on his face at the thought of Isabella anywhere near a wedding gown. Now, here he was sitting in a pew at her wedding, hoping that the bride would come to her senses and turn to him like she always desired to. The story played out well in his mind, but when he opened his eyes to see the reality of Isabella coming down the aisle in a dress for Raymond, his jaw tightened, and he bit his tongue. She looked like an angel in white with her dark hair cascading under the small veil she wore on her head. She was like a dream brought to life, and he desired to have every inch of her forever. He closed his eyes as he listened to the preacher speak, internally pleading that the moment would last forever and that Isabella would choose him, even now. The preacher asked if anyone disagreed with the marriage, and Lucas looked at Isabella with broken tears. To his surprise, she turned his way and looked straight into his gloomy green eyes. Her chocolate eyes glistened with tears. Lucas could sense the battle in her own heart, the one he wished to win long ago. He parted his lips and took a breath, but did not utter a word. Isabella turned back to Raymond, and the ceremony continued. Raymond slid a ring on her finger, and she slid one on his. They ended with a kiss to seal the marriage Lucas dreaded the most. Isabella had a gleaming glow about her that took his breath away, even after she was no longer his to claim. Lucas knew in his heart that their story was not over, and that there had to be a better end for him than solitary.

Chapter 6

After the rice was thrown, Irene walked up to her brother and sat with him. Their friends celebrated, but Irene could not bear the guilt if she did. She pushed her blond hair over her shoulders and blinked her eyelashes twice, looking for a way to speak with her brother. She watched him during their exit and noted his calm and collected state, but could also see his shattered selflessness as he watched the woman he loved make a horrible mistake. Irene smiled to the guests and smoothed over a perfect picture of happiness for her friend, but deep inside she was pleading with Isabella to run. Although, that choice had vanished the second she married Raymond Dailey. The day had been warm, but a sudden chill came over the town when Irene looked at her brother. "Stop being a wet blanket, Lucas."

He looked at her and almost instantly she felt regret for speaking with him. She put her hand on his shoulder and commented, "Lucas, you are hard boiled, but sometimes eggs break."

Lucas's eyes cut through Irene as he replied, "Don't compare my heart to an egg."

"Your heart is strong, you just need to believe in yourself. Live a life without her and you'll see."

"There's no life for me without Isabella," he replied as he stood to go. Irene shook her head. Her heart ached for her brother. Lucas was right about himself. All his life he had been with Isabella and to think of Lucas as a man without Isabella was frightening. An Isabella without Lucas was the most terrifying for Irene. She knew what kind of man Raymond was and regretted not telling Isabella the second she started carrying a torch for Raymond. The rice on the ground caught her eye, and a shot of immediate guilt erupted in her stomach. Irene knew that if anything happened to Isabella, she would be to blame.

Isabella pulled off her veil and shook her hair so that it fell naturally around her neck. She looked at Raymond, who had her in his arms, and felt as if the world had finally righted itself. She felt the strength of his hands and the calluses on his palms as she played with her ring. The car was nice, and she felt safe with Raymond at the wheel, although not as safe as she felt with Lucas. Her mind froze when Lucas crossed her mind. She could not feel safer with Lucas than she did with

Raymond. She could not feel anything for Lucas, because he was nothing but a friend. She closed her eyes and let out a sigh. The black interior of the car was strangely comforting, but confining nonetheless. She held her breath when the hotel was in sight, because she knew what was coming and was not sure she was ready for it. She knew if Lucas were there with her, everything would be all right. Then her mind shut off, and she knew she could not be thinking about Lucas.

Lucas sat up in his bed that night and watched the sky from his window. Unable to sleep, he prayed for Isabella and the life she was going to lead. He looked at the photograph he had of her and smiled at their innocent faces. He and Isabella were the most perfect people in New Orleans for one another. People were astonished they were not engaged, frankly, the town was shocked when they heard Isabella was engaged to a man other than Lucas. He wiped his cheeks as he opened the drawer to his nightstand to place the picture back in its rightful place. A small box caught his eye that was too familiar for his liking. He pulled it out to examine its contents. The soft box held a diamond ring, and in every inch, he saw Isabella Archer. He held it in his hands and pondered what he would do with it since Isabella could no longer be his wife. He brushed his hands through his dark hair as he remembered the day he purchased it. It was over seven years ago, and he had planned to propose to Isabella that day. He prepared vigorously and had planned their entire day, but that morning was the morning her parents passed away in an accident. They were eating breakfast together when a friend delivered the news, and they both dropped everything and ran into the hospital so Isabella could identify her parents. Lucas remembered hearing her heart crack as she clang to his shoulder for the strength she could not find in herself. He looked at the ring once more and put it back in its place, hopeful that he could use it again one day. Maybe he could sell it.

Isabella woke up the next morning with a content and radiant smile on her lips. She wiggled her toes and pointed her feet to stretch her tired muscles. She turned onto her left side and looked out of the window to see a busy street calling her name. Rubbing her eyes, Isabella looked at the time on the clock by her bed and saw that she had slept until eight o'clock, which was very out of character for her. She felt a panic in her chest and looked to her right to see Raymond lying next to her. As she watched him sleep, her thoughts began to race. The thought of marriage for Isabella had always centered around Lucas, and to think that she was laying in bed with her husband, who was not Lucas, was a strange feeling. She blinked her eyes and with them she blinked back her feelings. Lucas should not be on her mind, not now. Not ever. She laid back down and tried to sleep, but awoke when Raymond turned to her and said, "I love you, Isabella Dailey."

Isabella smiled back at him and swallowed her reservations as she looked into his comforting eyes. Raymond's dashing smile and warm eyes made her heart flutter. Blinking her chocolate eyes, she replied, "Good morning, dear."

He looked at her and sat up. "I'm going to go for a cup of joe. Do you want anything?"

She returned a caring glance and replied, "I'm fine. I'll see you after."

As Raymond left the hotel room, Isabella rushed from under the covers into the bathroom. She looked at herself intently in the mirror. Her dark curls fell from her head in a disheveled way. She noticed her eyes were watery, holding small tears that wept for the woman they knew she used to be. Isabella traced her lips with a pencil and dabbed her face with makeup. She slid into her low-waist dress that ruffled at the bottom. Isabella ran her hands down the red dress and looked at herself in the mirror once more before she left the bathroom to wait for Raymond to return. She took out her favorite book and read to pass the time.

Lucas poked his eggs with his fork with no appetite left to fulfill. He looked out his window to what was to him a dreary street. He watched the children play and felt a pulling ache in his chest as if the whole world had turned against him. Irene walked into the room with her hair in curls, but Lucas's glance did not waiver. He stared at the children on the street, hoping that he could jump into their happiness to escape his overwhelming darkness.

"They'll get cold," Irene said as she slammed her plate on the table.

Lucas looked at his sister with disappointed eyes, wondering why she could be so insensitive toward him. He shook his head and replied, "I don't have much of an appetite."

Looking into Irene's eyes, Lucas could see that she was disappointed in him for the way he had acted. However, he could also see a glimmer of sympathy in her blurred-morning sight. He took one bite of his eggs to please his sister, but then left the room as if he was running from a ghost.

Throwing his jacket over his shoulder with a briefcase in his other hand, Lucas walked out of the door and toward his work. He passed by the children he had looked at so intently from the window and his heartbeat slowed as he blended into his surroundings.

Work was tiresome that day, but it was all he had to distract himself from the thought of Isabella and Raymond. He flipped through a few faded papers on his desk and scratched his to-do list until there was nothing left to accomplish. Rubbing his eyes, Lucas began to type his feelings on the typewriter before him. He wished typing his emotions would bring Isabella back, but he gained control over himself as he wrote. His fingers glided over the keys as he pressed hard for the letters to stick. When his page was complete, he placed it in a folder and signed his name and the date. He sat for a moment and studied the wood on his desk, hoping to find answers there.

Lucas put his folder into his briefcase and buttoned his coat, preparing for the battles life had yet to bring him. He walked out into the streets of New Orleans as the night was falling down. He looked at the moon and the sun, both beautiful and both residing in the same sky. A small smile slid on his face as the sound of sweet slow jazz music touched his ears. Lucas smiled at the moon, sun, and stars, finding them lucky to be together under the same sky.

Chapter 7

Isabella looked outside to the bright light of day and smiled at the birds that flew past her window. To think that she and Raymond were married a year ago today was unbelievable, but Isabella had cherished every moment of the past year. She looked at her husband, who stood shaving in the bathroom, and a blank smile appeared on her face. Raymond was a fine man, and she loved him, but for Isabella something was missing. Maybe it was just a phase after the first year of marriage, but she felt as if it was something much more. Turning from her husband, she dressed for the day.

Raymond entered as she turned around in a deep blue dress that enhanced her chocolate eyes. She gave him a polite nod as he gave her a habitual kiss on the cheek and left for work.

Turning to a mirror, she put pearls in her ears and around her neck. With a touch of red lipstick, she licked her lips, cleaned her teeth, and began to tidy up the bedroom. She opened Raymond's cabinet drawer beside the bed to put away his books, and found a small bottle of liquid. Wondering if it was new cologne, she took a sniff. Her nostrils burned, and she quickly regretted the action. Isabella immediately identified the liquid as moonshine. Her heart stalled for a moment. She looked at the small glass bottle and realized that her suspicions of Raymond's differing behavior, and her uneasiness could stem from the very drink she hated. Isabella placed the drink back in her husband's cabinet, and hoped that he would not notice that she had found it.

Lucas sat at his desk, writing his every thought of Isabella down for safekeeping. Being a successful journalist with a great new column, Lucas spent most of his time at his desk. He loved the feeling he got after finishing a news piece. He always hoped that Isabella would be on the other side of the page, soaking up every word of his paper. He knew that was not very likely. Lucas rubbed his burning eyes and decided to see if his sister needed help setting the table for supper.

As Lucas walked through the door of his home, he was greeted by the smell of Irene's classic homemade apple pie. It was as if he was a young man again, just coming back from the park with Isabella by his side. Lucas rounded the corner and surprised Irene, who was just taking the pie out of their new oven. "May I help?"

Irene smiled at her brother and replied, "Set the table. Fred said he was coming over for supper."

"Very well," Lucas said as he began to set three spots at the table. Lucas liked Fred a great deal, and they always had a grand time when he came to visit Irene. He could tell by the twinkle in his sister's eye that they were getting serious. What Fred seemed to feel for Irene was a pure and honest love. Lucas placed the napkins down and laughed internally—that is the love he'll never feel.

Fred came to call shortly after the table was set. Lucas answered the door since Irene was elbow-deep in chicken. She came into the room to greet her guest, but hurried back to the kitchen to finish supper. Lucas was glad for it, because he could spend some time alone with his friend. He shook hands with Fred, but noticed that his friend's hands were shaking. He felt the strangest tension in the room. Fred slowly asked him to come look at his new car. Lucas agreed, but as they walked together he could see Fred's body grow more and more tense. Lucas placed his hand on the vehicle and commented, "She's a beauty, Fred."

"I purchased her yesterday. A new home too."

"Is that right?" Lucas asked with one eyebrow raised. He knew what question would follow.

"Sure is."

There was a long pause in the conversation. Lucas stared at the car's red color and waited for Fred to get up the courage to ask him for Irene's hand in marriage. The silent moment lasted longer. Lucas looked Fred straight in the eyes and asked, "I know you want to ask me something. What is it?"

Fred laughed nervously as he replied, "I was wondering if you would grant me permission to marry your sister."

Lucas rubbed his chin to make Fred sweat a little. Moments later he smiled. He shook Fred's hand, agreeing to let Fred propose to Irene.

They walked back up to the apartment and were welcomed by Irene and the wonderfully delicious supper she had prepared. The meal was quite uneventful and somewhat tense. Lucas could see Fred's desire to ask Irene for her hand in marriage, so he quickly excused himself after dessert. He sat in his room with the door cracked, listening to their conversation, and laughing along with Fred's ignorant remarks that only a man in love would utter. He watched as Fred took Irene's hand and got down on his knee. Tears swelled in his sister's eyes. She flung herself onto Fred after he placed a ring on her hand. Lucas gave them time together and ventured over to his typewriter to journal the events of the night. Someday, he would like to be the man in love proposing to his future wife—whoever she was.

Isabella paced through the kitchen, waiting for Raymond to return from work. He was usually late. Raymond was missing supper after supper the past few months. As she paced around her kitchen, Isabella's mind kept gong back to the half-empty bottle of moonshine she found under her husband's side table. The pasta boiled over the pot. Isabella quickly dumped the noodles into another bowl. When she tuned around, she heard the door close and saw Raymond's face looking blankly into her own. It was as if the man she once knew was no longer residing in his shell of a body. Isabella welcomed him home and confessed that she was worried about his late arrival. Raymond didn't listen and walked straight into their bedroom. Isabella followed him only to see him lying face down on their bed. She approached him slowly and asked, "Dear, are you ill?"

Raymond let out a sigh. "Get me coffee."

"It's suppertime, Raymond. We'll have no coffee until the morning," she gently replied as she placed her hand on his back. Raymond sat up slowly and began to slur his words, asking for the glass bottle in his cabinet. He said it was medicine he needed for his headache. Isabella refused to give it to him, knowing that drinking was illegal for start, and for second that being drunk was not an amiable quality. Isabella walked away from Raymond, but felt a tug on her arm. Raymond leaned close to her and demanded she hand him his bottle of liquor, but she refused. Raymond's face grew a deep shade of red Isabella had never seen before. He took his hand and slapped her across the back of her head. She sat at the edge of her bed, shocked by what had happened. She placed her hand on her throbbing head and tried to get free of Raymond's grip. He refused to let go. He continued to hit her with his fists until she obey him. She reached for the bottle and handed it to her husband. Her head was pounding, but Isabella was still in shock of what was taking place. She felt numb and afraid, praying someone would show up to her home. After Raymond finished off what was left in the container, he demanded for more.

"There's no more Raymond."

Raymond was not the kind of man to take no for an answer. He took the glass bottle and slung it across the room. The shards fell on her foot, making hundreds of small incisions.

Isabella covered her face to protect it and meekly walked out of the room. She stumbled into the extra room and locked the door behind her. Her arm felt broken, and her head felt like it had shattered. Isabella pushed the bed and vanity against the door. She hoped that if Raymond went searching for her, the furniture would detain him long enough for her to make an escape out the window. Isabella looked in the vanity mirror and saw her face begin to change from a creamy white to a reddish color. Then, it swelled. Her arm ached more as she realized that her side was also sore from the reprimand she had just received. Isabella crawled to the corner of the room and placed her ear on the wall adjacent to her and Raymond's room. She heard him upchuck two or three times that night, but she did not move a muscle. She had no desire to help him. With her legs against her chest, and the beat of her heart in her ears, Isabella stayed awake for the remainder of the night, hoping that Raymond had fallen asleep and wanted no more of her.

Isabella heard noises from the adjacent room. She sat silently as she heard her husband get ready for work. She did not move, in fear he would hear her. The door closed. She heard the car pull out of the driveway. Isabella sighed in relief. Her mind was spinning, and her body felt as if it had been run over. She made her way to the vanity and looked in the mirror only to see that the red marks had turned a deep blue-purple. She lifted her blouse and saw that her ribs were splattered with blue marks as well. Her arm was better, but it also had faint streaks of blue. Isabella thought about running, but did not know where to run.

A few hours later, she heard a car pull into the driveway. Her heartbeat raced when she heard footsteps coming closer to the home. She was ready to defend herself with a knife she had found in an old set of silverware that had been stored in the closet. She heard a knock on the door, which was strange. Isabella pushed the furniture away from the door and slowly peaked out to see if Raymond was home. She made a dash for the door and opened it. To her pleasant surprise it was Lucas Matthews.

Isabella dropped her knife and melted into his resistant arms. Lucas held Isabella as tenderly as he could without being too affectionate. He heard her faint cries and felt them in his chest. Lucas was certainly not prepared for this kind of greeting from his old friend.

He took Isabella's shoulders and gently pushed her away from him. He saw the bruises on her face and arms, and his eyes grew wider than the gulf. He stood silent for a moment, not knowing what to say. He placed his hands under Isabella's chin and examined her face, horrified someone would do this to her. He looked into her chocolate eyes and saw nothing but paralyzing fear. "Who did this to you?"

She looked into his eyes for the first time in a year. "Raymond."

Lucas tried to control his anger as he helped her into his car. He looked at the woman he loved and took a deep breath to temper his utter disgust for her husband.

The drive to the apartment was quiet. Lucas had not seen Isabella since the wedding and could not help but feel guilty about what happened to her. He looked at her profile and came to realize that what she needed was security. She also needed a woman to talk with.

Isabella remained silent as Lucas helped her up the stairs and into his apartment. Irene was there, for which she was very grateful. Irene had the same blank expression as Lucas when he first saw her. Isabella was ashamed of her appearance, but was more ashamed at her inability to speak. She was in shock. Irene quickly took her from Lucas, who was explaining all he knew. Irene took Isabella's hand and instructed her brother to keep watch as she helped Isabella undress and wash. The warm water felt good on Isabella's sore body. She washed herself, but needed help getting into some of Irene's casual clothing. Irene talked with her and comforted her, but Isabella could not say a word. It was like her mouth was wired shut. Isabella slept with Irene that night. She was grateful to have her friends watching over her. Nonetheless, every time Isabella closed her eyes she saw Raymond's steaming red face.

Chapter 8

I sabella looked out of the apartment window, curled up in a chair with a blanket wrapped around her body. She heard Lucas behind her and let out a sigh. Irene had business to tend to that day, so Lucas was charged with watching her. Lucas must hate her, or he at least resented her. No matter how Lucas felt, she was grateful for the two weeks she had had with the Matthews. Lucas handed her warm tea and sat next to her in a chair opposite hers. Isabella looked at him as he gazed toward the sunrise, rubbing his hands together. She sipped her tea slowly as she laid her eyes on the same pink sky.

"Is it good?" Lucas asked as he gestured toward the glass in her hand.

"Yes, thank you," she replied with a small smile. Isabella looked out the window and commented, "Thank you for coming when you did."

"It was no bother. I was glad to be of help."

"Why were you there?"

"Something told me to check up on you."

"Something?"

"We had not heard from you in a while. I was worried."

Isabella looked over and watched him sip his coffee. Lucas's mind seemed to be in another place in time, a place Isabella wished to escape to. Any place would be better than where she was. His green eyes were lighter than she remembered, and his wrinkles had certainly begun to show more than they had before. He looked exhausted.

"I wouldn't give him the moonshine I found in his side table."

Lucas turned to face Isabella.

"After he hit me a while I got it for him. He wanted more, and I didn't have any so he got even more enraged and threw the bottle at me."

Lucas leaned closer. His eyebrows came together to form an apathetic frown.

"I hid in the next room and waited until he left. I couldn't move."

"What he did to you is inexcusable. Isabella, you deserve better."

She blinked back her tears. "He's my husband, Lucas."

Lucas placed his coffee on the small table in front of them and took both her hands in his. His warm hands were strong and made Isabella feel as if he could protect her from anything. "I can't watch him hurt you like this, Isabella. You know you're a friend, correct? I would never want to jeopardize what you have with him, but could you stay a while? It would be best for you, and give him time to cool off. You could collect yourselves."

Isabella gave a small smile and replied, "Yes, thank you, Lucas. Actually, I'm not ready to go back there just yet."

Lucas let go of her hands when he heard Irene's happy humming coming toward the front door. He sipped his coffee and returned to look at the bright streets. He could not stand what Raymond was doing. It bothered every inch of him when he looked at Isabella's bruises. Irene came into the apartment cheerfully with groceries in her hand. She placed them in the kitchen and commented, "Breakfast will be ready shortly."

"Actually, Lucas, I have to tell you something," Isabella stated.

Lucas got up from the chair and left Isabella alone. He took his jacket from the coatrack and informed the women, "Tell me when I return. I'm going to town. I'll be back shortly."

After Lucas left, Irene looked at Isabella and blatantly asked, "What was that?"

"I don't know."

"Where's he going?"

"Beats me."

Irene looked at her friend with apathy in her eyes. Isabella smiled and commented, "I agreed to stay here awhile until I heal and Raymond cools off."

Irene turned around to unload her groceries and to hide her guilty tears. "Good."

Lucas slammed the car door as he looked at Isabella and Raymond's small home. It had a strange feel to it, the house—almost a ghostly feel. Lucas straightened his coat and thought of what he would say to Raymond. He never liked Raymond, and now Lucas knew why he had a sickening feeling about Isabella's attachment to him. Lucas knocked on the faded gray door and waited for a response, trying to keep a cool head. The door opened. Raymond revealed himself through the small crack in the door. Lucas looked into his jaded and watery eyes. Lucas could smell a potent pathetic scent of booze and salt. "I want no trouble, Raymond."

The door opened wider. Raymond wore a stained undershirt. Lucas scrunched his nose and took off his fashionable hat. "Look, Raymond, Isabella's with us. I thought you should know."

"Figures she would run to you. I was only a little upset," Raymond replied with a wipe of his nose and a swig of alcohol.

Lucas burned with anger, but he tried to play it off with a smile. "Did you see her face, Raymond?"

"I see that woman's face everyday."

Lucas clenched his fists. "She was beaten up pretty bad and honestly, I'm not sure she's safe here. Not to mention, what you're drinking is strictly illegal."

He regretted his last sentence when Raymond's face grew tense. Raymond threw his bottle on the ground and replied,

"That woman's my wife, and I demand you bring her back here at once."

Lucas lost his self-control. "That woman has a name and that woman is more than property you can parade around and command at your leisure. That woman is intelligent, thoughtful, graceful, caring, and understanding. These are the only reasons I presume she would come back to a boozehound like you, and I hope she learns sooner than later that a man like you is a poison and a danger to her and everyone else around. You're a weak and cowardly man!"

Lucas picked up the slightly cracked bottle of liquor on the front porch and forced it into Raymond's arms. "Good day, sir."

As Lucas drove home, he contemplated how he could persuade Isabella from going back to her husband. He knew that she would try to patch things up with Raymond. How he wished he could take Isabella away like he should have long ago. How he wished he could take back his idleness and reach out for Isabella, his dearest friend and first love. His only love. As he rounded the corner to the apartment, he saw Isabella and Irene embrace. Fred shook his head with a smile on his face. Lucas was glad that Isabella had good news to focus on—that her closest friend was engaged and soon to be married. He hoped that this news would delay her return to Raymond.

Isabella gave Lucas a memorable smile as he entered the apartment. She wrapped her arms around his neck. "Is this not the best news of the year?"

"I dare say it is," Lucas replied.

Isabella was comforted by his voice. The four friends sat in the living room as Irene described in detail how Fred proposed to her. Isabella was captivated by her story and was filled with giddy smiles. Then, the attention turned to her as Lucas asked, "What was it you wanted to tell me?"

Isabella's hands grew cold, and she grasped the sides of the couch. Isabella was happy that Lucas had made it home in time to hear the announcement she had been hiding for the past weeks. She was nervous that Lucas would make a scene. Lucas hated Raymond, and with a good cause. Isabella saw that now. That did not change the fact that Raymond was her husband and that she desired to mend things with him. Isabella replied, "I've decided to go back to Raymond."

Isabella watched as Lucas's eyes grew smaller. He sat for a moment in silence, which, she knew, was a bad sign. Isabella looked at Irene, who seemed just as speechless as her brother. Fred, being one of the more rational people in the group, asked, "Why? You just agreed to stay here."

Irene put her hand on his as if to silence him, knowing that this was really a conversation between Lucas and Isabella. Isabella wished Lucas would understand. She knew that he would try to. It was in that moment that Isabella Archer realized that she was more than just an old friend to him. She and Lucas had shared something special in adolescence, but to think that he still felt the same was startling. It was also comforting, and the worst part was that she felt it too.

"Why?"

"He's my husband, Lucas, you know that," she said as he tenderly took her hand. "I have to go back."

Lucas leaned closer to her and pleaded, "Isabella, he's not the same man you married."

"Yes, but I married him."

"His true character has revealed itself. Isabella, I want you to be safe."

"I'm supposed to be safe with *him*, Lucas."

"But you're not safe there."

"I have to be."

Lucas rubbed his hands together as Isabella's heart broke. She wanted to stay, but knew she had a duty to her husband.

"You could stay here, and we could protect you from him. Maybe you could…"

"I'm pregnant, Lucas," Isabella interrupted, stopping Lucas's painful rambling.

Isabella looked at Irene and Fred, who immediately left the room.

Lucas's eyebrows softened when tears fell down Isabella's cheeks. Her shaking hands were proof that she was terrified and needed all of the support he could give her. Lucas wiped her tears and replied, "Congratulations."

Her tears grew. "I want my baby to be safe, but I can't leave him."

Lucas welcomed her embrace and slowly rubbed her back to comfort her. "Isabella, I will protect you as much as

I can. You can both survive this." Isabella drew back from him, and he took her shoulders, looking into her eyes. "You're strong and brave, and your love for this child will protect it from harm."

Isabella wiped her own tears as she faked a smile. "Thank you, Lucas."

Four months later, Isabella was feeling much better. It was nice that Raymond was never home. It made the pregnancy easier to hide from him. Isabella had not yet told Raymond about the baby, because she wanted to try to work on their marriage first. That idea was not as easily carried out. Raymond was too hooked on his drinking. Isabella was noticing that her clothes were starting to show she was pregnant. She tried to hide it with loose shirts and dresses, but it was getting impossible to cover. She would have to tell him soon. Tonight.

Isabella tucked one of Raymond's shirts on the line to dry as he walked into the home, fresh for once. He had no smell of liquor on him, and Isabella determined that now would be the best time to tell him about her pregnancy. She cooked dinner and served her husband, like usual. They had a mild conversation. It was harder to tell Raymond, the father of her child, about her pregnancy than it was to tell Lucas. She knew there was something wrong with that fact. Isabella had no idea how Raymond would respond, and could only hope he was excited about the new addition. She gathered the courage to speak. Then, the news came out of her mouth like a bullet would fire out of a gun. Raymond dropped his fork. Isabella tried to read him for a reaction.

"What?"

"We're going to have a baby," she tried to proclaim with enthusiasm.

"You're joking."

Isabella was startled by his blank expression. "No, I'm four months along."

"Four months? Why did you not say anything?"

"I just didn't know how to."

With a huff Raymond replied, "I can't believe this, Isabella. I don't want it…We cannot afford it."

"It's a baby, not a new car or moonshine, Raymond," Isabella retorted without censoring her thoughts.

Raymond raised his voice. "What did you say?"

"It's a child, Raymond, something to rejoice over."

"They have ways to get rid of it."

Isabella was taken aback by her husband's suggestion and violently shook her head. She got up from the table and tried to go to their room to process what her husband was suggesting. As she left, Raymond followed her screaming, "We cannot care for another mouth, Isabella! I'm already working to feed yours, and then you blame *me* for needing an escape from *you*."

"I had no idea I was such a burden to you, Raymond. Maybe you should just kill me instead, and get rid of all your troubles at once! But wait, we cannot forget about your precious liquor! Well, I threw it out! With no liquor to help you along you would not dare harm me or our child."

Raymond slapped Isabella across the face, knocking her off her feet. With each punch, she fought Raymond harder and harder. Eventually, she knocked him out with a long piece of wood she had stored in case of an emergency. Fearing he had broken one of her ribs, Isabella struggled to get to the other room. She climbed out of the window and into the car, because she knew she could not walk to Lucas and Irene's home. With fear and adrenaline rushing through her veins, Isabella made it to Lucas and Irene's in a perfect amount of time. She crawled up the stairs to reach their door, all the while feeling as if there was a sharp knife sticking out of her abdomen.

Irene answered the door, and Isabella let out a sigh of relief when she saw her friend's familiar face. Irene helped her to her bed and tried to make her comfortable. Isabella tried to tell Irene what happened, but fainted shortly after she saw Lucas enter the room.

Lucas looked at Isabella and immediately called for a midwife. He returned to Irene's room and saw tearstains on Isabella's face. The red bruises were beginning to appear on her arms and legs. He leaned in closer and watched as Irene tried to feel for the baby.

"Is it okay?" Lucas asked.

"I don't know. Did you call the midwife?"

"She'll be here in an hour," Lucas replied as tears began to fall off his face. He paced back and forth outside the room, trying to piece together what might have happened. He blamed himself for letting Isabella return to Raymond so soon. He knew that he would have to do everything within his power to keep Isabella at his home until the baby was born.

The midwife arrived an hour later, and examined Isabella and listened to the baby. She informed Irene and Lucas that Isabella had bad bruising and no broken bones, but for the baby's sake, she needed to stay at rest until she healed. Lucas was thankful that Isabella had to remain there for another month or two, because she and the baby would be out of danger and away from Raymond.

Chapter 9

A month later, a healed Isabella helped Irene into her wedding gown. It was something Isabella had always dreamed of doing. Isabella wore a sky-blue, knee-length dress and pearls that dipped in front of her rather-large stomach. Isabella was glad that she was able to stay with Irene as she healed. Isabella was too invested in Irene's wedding to think of anything else during her stay, especially Raymond. As girls, she and Irene would dream up weddings for one another, Isabella for Irene and Fred, and Irene for Isabella and Lucas. As Isabella reminisced, her heart sunk. She dropped a tube of lipstick and tried to pick it up, but abandoned the idea. She always thought she would marry Lucas. Nonetheless, there she was, married and with child. Isabella let out a nervous laugh and picked up the lipstick with her toes as if nothing had happened. The hairdresser noticed her shaking hands and asked, "Are you nervous?"

"Not particularly. Anyway, it's Irene's wedding."

The woman fixed her glasses with one hand and touched Isabella's hand with her other. She was older, about sixty, and was kind to look at, even at her age.

"The baby," the woman commented.

Isabella looked to see if Irene was otherwise occupied. She leaned in closer as if she was whispering feral gossip. "Very. My husband is…well…it's complicated, you see…"

She tried to hold back her tears as the kind woman placed her hands under her chin. "My dear, you'll be a great mother. Husband or not."

Isabella smiled and thanked the lady for her encouraging words. Irene came to sit beside her. Her dress was exquisite; it was white with feathers, and pearls draped down her torso.

As the wedding chapel filled, Lucas looked around for Raymond. He hoped that Raymond would not attempt to make an appearance. He had never come for Isabella, which Lucas found very odd. If Isabella was his wife and had gone missing for a month, he would search the world to find her. Lucas concluded that this was the difference in men like him and men like Raymond. Lucas closed the backdoors and turned around to see Isabella and his sister walking toward him. They were both beautiful—on the inside and as equally so on the outside. The blue dress Isabella wore brought out her chocolate eyes. She made Lucas feel as if he was ice cream being sold on a warm day in August. His sister looked majestic, and it took much self-control for Lucas to hold back his happy tears. Isabella smiled at him with a hint of water in her eyes. "Is she not the most beautiful woman in New Orleans?"

Wanting to say that he thought her the second most beautiful, Lucas smiled and nodded at Isabella's comment. The chapel doors opened, and Isabella and Fred's sisters walked out in a line. Lucas looked at his sister, his baby sister, and hugged her before it was their turn to walk down the aisle arm in arm. Giving his sister away was one of the hardest and most honorable things Lucas had ever experienced.

All the same, giving up Isabella was much harder, because Lucas knew he would always have a place in his sister's heart. He was not sure if he still had a place in Isabella's. They were still cordial and kind to one another. Nevertheless, Lucas felt a pull on his heart to watch over Isabella, even if she thought she knew what she was doing.

After the wedding, Isabella and Lucas walked up to the apartment together. It felt strange for Isabella to know that she would be sleeping in the same apartment with a man other than her husband. The idea of being alone with Lucas sounded sweeter than any honey that had ever danced across her lips. Lucas must have been furious with her for getting herself into the situation she was in. If anything, she knew he pitied her. There would always be a space in her heart for

Lucas Matthews, if only there was a space left in his heart for her. She concluded that space was filled years ago.

Lucas said good night as soon as they walked in the door and escaped into his room. Isabella was afraid she had said something wrong, but figured it was the emotional day that was eating at Lucas. Isabella looked into the mirror and saw the bump on her once-flat stomach. This was supposed to be a happy time. Isabella tried to remember a time when she knew true happiness. It would have to have been the few hours before her parents passed away. Isabella had spent an entire morning with Lucas, seeing a performance in town the night before, and eating breakfast with one another. It was back when they were more than friends. Isabella smiled as she remembered the sun on her shoulders that day. It was beautiful. The sun had not shown as bright since then. The memory of the warm sun brought her back in time. There she was with Lucas, sipping tea and laughing at his impression of the French waiter they had the previous evening. Her memories halted when she heard a knock on her door. Lucas was on the other side. "Are you all right?"

Isabella opened the door slowly and let Lucas into what used to be Irene's room. Lucas put his hands on his hips and let out a sigh. "I suppose this is strange for the both of us."

Isabella looked confused, and Lucas knew that this idea was probably not the best. Even so, he continued, "You have to tell me something, Isabella. I have to know something."

Lucas continued to pace as Isabella sat on the bed. Lucas was more nervous now than he was walking his sister down the aisle just hours before. He rubbed his hands together and asked point-blank, "Do you love him?"

"He's my husband."

"I asked if you love him."

Lucas sat next to her on the bed and waited for her faint, "No."

It came, and when it did, Lucas tuned to look at her. He could see that she was very confused, but it was something he needed to hear. Maybe it was selfish and foolish, but Lucas needed the small flicker of hope to confront Raymond once again, as he planned to the following day. He smiled at Isabella and patted her on the back, not sure what other way to show her affection.

When Lucas left the room, Isabella dressed for the night and slowly crawled into the bed. She was still sore on her sides from her last incident, but was not concerned with any other pain but her emotional injuries. Isabella knew she would have to return to her husband within the next week, but was frightened for herself and her unborn child. She wished she was able to stay with Lucas, but knew that Lucas would not want her around for too much longer, especially after the child came. She thought back to Lucas's rash and prying question, and was confused. Nonetheless, the questions made her feel comfortable. It was as if they were close friends again.

The next morning, Lucas closed his door gently, hoping not to awake Isabella. He poured himself a cup of black coffee and picked up a newspaper. He turned to his article and smiled, thinking that if he could only publicize what was happening to his dear friend, he could stop her misery. He slipped out of the apartment and made his way to his car, reading the morning news he helped create the day before. Lucas noticed a spelling error and laughed at himself. He was never good at spelling. He tried to keep his head on straight as he drove toward Raymond. He wanted to politely plead in Isabella's defense.

Lucas knocked on the door when he arrived at Raymond's home. There was an extra vehicle in the front yard. He figured it was a colleague from Raymond's work, but then remembered Raymond's termination. It was in the paper three weeks back. Lucas brought his hand to his chin, and tried to piece together whose automobile could be sitting next to Raymond's.

It took a while, but eventually Raymond answered the door in nothing but an undershirt and underpants. It was something Lucas did not wish or expect to see. Lucas buttoned his coat and asked Raymond, "How do you do?"

"Mighty fine," Raymond answered with his hip blocking the door.

"I came here to talk about Isabella. She's doing well and so is the baby. I thought you might want to know."

As Raymond wiped his nose, there was a female giggle from behind the door. Lucas tried to look into the home, but Raymond refused to let him see the woman behind him.

"You better come back," Raymond replied as he tried to close the door.

Lucas raised his eyebrows, offended by Raymond's lack of respect for his wife. Lucas stopped the door and pushed it open. He saw a woman in a robe and liquor bottles surrounding the two in their clouds of smoke. Lucas looked at the woman and gestured to Raymond, "You do know he's married."

The woman made no reply, but gathered her things and retreated into Raymond and Isabella's room. Lucas turned to see Raymond gulp down more liquor. He took the bottle from Raymond and placed it on the table beside him. "Raymond, get your head where it needs to be."

"My head is right where it needs to be," Raymond replied as he picked up another bottle.

Lucas's anger had simmered to a boil. "Listen, dewdropper, you have no job, no prospects, and you're having an affair on your wife. You might just lose her and your baby. Now, you better know your onions! Figure out what's going on here and fix it. Isabella is going to hear about this woman you are with- I will make sure of it."

Raymond rolled his eyes, which made Lucas all the more frustrated. "Lucas, my friend, level with me." Raymond placed his arm around Lucas's shoulder. "Are you not having an affair with my wife?"

Lucas removed Raymond's hand immediately, retorting, "I'd never have an affair with anyone's wife. Isabella is my friend, and I'm trying to do right by her for her health and the health of the baby. She would not be in this situation if it weren't for you."

Raymond laughed with a sinful grin on his chapped lips. "Then, you won't mind me telling her you're still in love with her. She'd understand."

Lucas flinched, realizing that a man like Raymond was not worth his time or energy. He tipped his head to Raymond as if to say a forever farewell. He slammed the door and walked to his car. He had hoped that by being kind to Raymond, Raymond would gain back a sense of empathy for Isabella. Lucas got into his car and banged the steering wheel. Raymond was hopeless. Lucas knew what he had to do. His personal feelings for Isabella were a sacrifice he might have to make for Isabella and her baby's safety.

Chapter 10

Isabella was eight months' pregnant, and she was ready to be back home. She and Lucas had pleasant days together, and Irene came often to visit. It was not a few months after her wedding that Irene delivered the news that she was also expecting a child. Isabella was enthralled to hear the news. Irene suggested that if they had a boy and girl they would do everything in their power to match the two together. It was a grand thing to think about as Isabella approached the date of her return home to Raymond. She needed all of the positive thoughts she could get. Isabella was ready to return to regular life, but was still afraid of who Raymond had become. Lucas came back looking very concerned, as usual. Isabella could not tell if Lucas was now just a worried person or if there was something to be worried about. She hoped it was the first option.

Isabella did want to hear from Raymond and had begun to become suspicious as to why he had not called or written to her. She figured he was busy trying to obtain another job, and she did not want to put more stress on him than was necessary.

Lucas had sat down with Isabella a few times and tried to tell her something, but he could never let the words out of his mouth. So it was not surprising to Isabella when Lucas walked into the apartment that night and asked if they could talk. Isabella looked at her friend, concerned he had done something wrong. Lucas had visited Raymond the previous night. She sat down to listen.

Lucas seemed more nervous now than he was that day years ago when they went to breakfast. He sat down and blurted out the words, "Raymond's having an affair."

Isabella was speechless. Was that why he never came to call? Was Lucas making it up? Then again, why would Lucas make it up? Her mind stopped there, because the reason why Lucas would make it up scared her more than the fact that Raymond was having an affair. Lucas could not love her. It was impossible. She could not still feel the same. It was improbable.

"How do you know?"

Isabella could see that Lucas was struggling to tell her the truth, almost like it hurt him more than it would hurt her. "I saw him with another woman when I visited him yesterday. I didn't know how to tell you." Isabella's eyes watered. "I didn't want you to get hurt."

Isabella sat still and focused on her breathing. Should she leave Raymond? She wanted to leave him. At the same time, Isabella wanted to respect her marriage. People could change. She knew this from experience. Raymond was once kind and compassionate, and she was sure he could find those traits in himself again. She had to return as soon as possible and work with Raymond on his drinking. Maybe if she could fix his drinking problem, she could fix everything else it had affected.

"I have to go back."

"He hurt you bad last time, Isabella, he'll hurt you again. Maybe worse this time."

Isabella put her hand on Lucas's and clarified, "He's still my husband, Lucas, and I must do what's right. We must try to fix this, together, as husband and wife."

Lucas let out a soft and familiar laugh, "Are you a poet now?"

A small grin formed on his lips as his eyes reflected a small bittersweet sentiment. Isabella wished she could renounce her marriage and confess her love for Lucas in that moment, but she knew that she must try to mend things with Raymond. She must choose to love him.

Later that day, Lucas helped Isabella out of the automobile and to her front door. He rubbed his hand across hers as he asked one last time, "Are you sure?"

Isabella's tears said no, but her facade of a smile said yes. Lucas helped her with her bag and knocked on the door, hoping to find Raymond decent for a change. As the door opened, he saw a clean-shaven, suit-wearing, gentleman-looking Raymond at the door. He was a picture from the past, but the man of the past was no longer present. Lucas helped Isabella into the home and placed her bag in her room. He hoped that Isabella would always remember she could call him or Irene in any emergency. He reminded her before he left.

After Lucas left, things were strange with Raymond. The two had not spoken in months, and Isabella was still frightened by his temper. She politely suggested he try to give up the liquor, and he was supportive—finally pointing out that it was illegal anyway. Isabella was glad he finally noted this obvious fact. Isabella was surprised at how different Raymond was and how much he seemed like the man she once loved. She hoped she could learn to love him again. If anything, she could learn to tolerate him if he kept his hands off her.

Isabella cleaned the kitchen, which had not been cleaned in months. There were still dishes left over from her last meal with Raymond. She found it revolting. After she fixed the kitchen, she tried to move the furniture in the spare room. Isabella then decided it was best for the baby that she remain calm. Being eight months' pregnant was exciting, but it made everyday tasks more complicated.

After a week at home with Raymond, the two decided to take an outing with their friends. It was a way to show them they were working everything out. Isabella sat in a lawn chair beside her husband with Irene, Fred, and Lucas across the table from her. The park was clean, thankfully. Isabella was happy to be back with her husband, planning outings with friends, and preparing for the child. However, there was a sickening feeling she got in the pit of her stomach when her eyes connected with Raymond's. It was as if there was something missing in his eyes; something that had disappeared over the past three years. It was now early spring of 1927, but Isabella felt as if she was still stuck in 1925. As Irene talked about possible names for her baby, Isabella nodded politely and gave her input when the time felt right.

"Do you have names?" Irene asked Raymond as she sipped on her lemonade.

Isabella felt Raymond's finger tap her shoulder as he replied, "I'm sure Isabella has thought one up."

"Alexander if a boy and Doris if a girl."

Irene choked on her lemonade, and Lucas shot a hot glance toward Isabella. Raymond seemed oblivious, but Irene, Isabella, and Lucas all knew that Doris was Lucas and Irene's mother's name. Alexandra was Isabella's mother's name. Isabella and Lucas's eyes met for a moment, and she saw the gratitude he was trying to convey to her. Isabella came to realize in that moment that she was a firm believer that once you love someone, you can never let that person blur back into the nothingness they were before you met them. Isabella would have to try and cope with her marriage to Raymond and turn the love she felt for Lucas into a brotherly love. She sipped her lemonade as the gentlemen dismissed themselves to play ball.

Irene looked at Isabella with a small smile on her lips. "I'm happy to see you and Raymond working things out."

Isabella turned her head to Irene. "He has not touched liquor since I moved back in a few weeks ago, and he controls his temper well."

"That's good to hear. You know, Lucas seems to be doing well too."

Isabella ignored Irene's comment about Lucas and replied, "How do you feel?"

"The headaches stopped. Lucas said…"

"Please, stop."

"Stop what?" Irene looked at Isabella as if she was a crazy person just let out of the asylum.

"I don't want to talk about Lucas, please."

Isabella looked at Irene, pleading. Irene was getting suspicious as to why she did not care to talk about Lucas. Irene was a good friend, Isabella knew, and would not ask a question for which she was not ready to hear the answer. Irene had always hoped Isabella and Lucas would marry. In fact, years ago, Irene predicted they would be engaged by the time they were both twenty-five. Isabella let out a small laugh, noting how wrong Irene was on that assumption.

Lucas passed the ball to Fred, and they scored a point for their team. Raymond patted him on the back and congratulated him on the pass. It was strange for Lucas to be playing ball with Raymond. Maybe it was not the man he hated, but what the man had become. They took a break to devise a plan of action. The other team took a substantial amount of time, which left their team plenty of time to talk. Lucas avoided conversations with Raymond as much as possible, because Raymond never spared a moment to parade the fact that he was married to Isabella.

"Isabella's doing well these days," Raymond commented for no particular reason.

"Good," Fred replied. Lucas was thankful Fred was there to keep the peace between him and Raymond.

"Yesterday, she was fixing breakfast and our baby started to move, so she accidentally dropped the glasses. You should've seen her face."

"I suppose she was thrilled to feel the little one kick," Fred replied as he wiped his sweat. Lucas held his tongue.

"She's always dropping things now. I suppose it was the spill she took a few months back that weakened her arm. I love her."

Lucas was slow to anger, but he could not control the pure righteous anger he felt toward Raymond. The nerve to talk about the woman he once used as a punching bag and say that he loved her!

"Please, let's talk about something else," Lucas gently suggested.

Raymond came toward Lucas and raised his voice, "Are you mad because your friend happens to be my wife?"

Lucas was taken aback by Raymond's comment, not expecting that harsh of a response. Fred stepped between the two. "Calm down here."

"No, I'd like to know what was happening to my wife while she was staying alone with her 'friend,'" Raymond replied as he nudged Fred out of the way.

Lucas swallowed and replied, "Nothing. I gave her a home when she had none. I cared for her as I would've cared for any orphan or widow. I swear."

"My wife is not an orphan or widow, sir."

Lucas shook his head and replied with a soft tone, "Your wife is an orphan, Raymond. Your wife lost her parents years ago, so, yes. I cared for her because she had nowhere to go. I cared for her, because her husband was too drunk to differentiate her from exercise equipment."

Raymond snarled at Lucas, shaking his head. Lucas tried to keep himself from swooping Isabella away from her abusive and narcissistic husband. Before Lucas could do anything for Isabella, Raymond had her in his arms and in the car. The other two men slowly returned to the table.

"What was that?" Irene asked her brother as he and Fred approached her.

He rolled his eyes and sighed. "Raymond, as usual."

Lucas grabbed Irene's things. Fred shook his head. He took his wife's hand and commented, "I've never seen a more angry man."

Irene gave her husband a kind reminder. "He doesn't have faith. I fear neither of them do."

Lucas put on his sweater and replied, "Isabella does, I know." Lucas looked at his sister and asked, "If anything should happen to Isabella and she needs a place to stay, could she stay with you?"

Irene gave her brother a quick hug as she replied, "Yes."

Isabella waited outside the store for Raymond to reenter the car. She saw him behind the building and hoped he was not acting strange because of the brown bag he held in his hand. He probably was. The day was lovely, so why would Raymond be buying liquor again? He made a promise. After finishing one bottle, he purchased another one and made his way back to the car. His speech was a little muffled, and his reflexes were impaired, but Isabella did not want to fight with him, not while he had a bottle in his hand. She knew better.

When they got home, Isabella took a shower with the bathroom door locked, knowing what the night ahead might look like. She hoped she was wrong, but Isabella always knew Raymond's fists would find her again. After she was dressed, she made her way out of the bathroom and into the bedroom where Raymond sat, drunk. He looked like he wanted to fight.

Isabella slipped into the bed and prayed Raymond would fall asleep. He left the room, and Isabella sat up, paralyzed and concerned. She did not want him to hurt her baby. If anything were to happen, she had to save her child, no matter the cost. An hour passed, and she heard the front door open and close. She eventually fell asleep waiting on Raymond to return home.

Isabella woke up with a stinging sensation across her cheek. Her eyes met Raymond's, and she fought her way away from him. She tried to defend herself, but he was too powerful and too intoxicated. Isabella prayed that God would deliver her from his fists and into His sweet embrace, but Isabella knew she could not leave her child alone in the world with Raymond. She kicked Raymond where she knew it would hurt, but not before he hit her in the stomach. She struck Raymond with the same piece of wood as before and crawled to the phone, dialing for the police. They said they were coming. She hung up to call Lucas. She dialed the number and heard his worried tone on the other end of the line. Isabella began to scream when she felt a pain worse than any broken bone. She begged Lucas to come to her. "Lucas, The baby is coming!"

Chapter 11

Lucas made it to her home before the officials and immediately called for a midwife. With no money to pay for a doctor, Lucas knew a midwife was the only choice. He looked at Isabella's terrified face and searched the home for Raymond. He had vanished. Lucas rushed to Isabella's side and tried to keep her calm. When the midwife came, she asked Lucas to hold Isabella up as she pushed.

An hour later, baby Doris came into the world. She looked just like Isabella, or at least Lucas thought she did. He held Isabella as she held her baby girl. There was no place Lucas would rather have been in that moment than with the two most precious women he knew. Lucas brushed Isabella's hair out of her face so he could see the child. He was breathless at the sight of the new life. Isabella handed baby Doris to Lucas as the midwife helped her shower and change clothes.

He did not mind the alone time with baby Doris. In fact, he treasured it.

He rocked her in his arms and sang to her as she cried. It would not be the first time she would cry. Lucas prayed that any crying she had in the future would be a result of tired eyes, empty stomachs, and lost toys. He prayed that Doris would inspire each of them to live to the fullest. Lucas looked at the beautiful baby girl and vowed to love and protect her as his own for the rest of his life. Someone had to promise her that much.

Isabella slipped on her slippers and thanked the woman for helping her change. The woman smiled and commented, "It seems like your husband's already captivated by her."

Isabella blushed. "That's not my husband." The woman looked at Isabella with a raised eyebrow. "My husband's away on work and asked Lucas to care for me."

Isabella was helped to her bed, and the woman excused herself to get Lucas and to clean the mess left behind. As Isabella waited for Lucas to enter with her baby, she laid her head on her soft pillow. Isabella knew that everything happened for a reason. Maybe the end of her trials had come through this new addition to their family. Maybe she needed the trials to make her stronger for Doris's sake. Isabella knew God had a plan for her and her baby. She opened her eyes as Lucas entered the room with Doris in his arms. "I think she wants her mother."

Isabella took Doris in her arms and touched her small nose. Her small fingers grasped Isabella's and a tear of relief spilled over Isabella's eyes. She knew that as long as she had Doris with her, everything would turn out fine.

Lucas touched Doris's stomach and tickled it. "I think she likes it here."

Isabella smiled at Lucas and felt the same warm pull in her chest she felt when she first saw Doris. She touched Lucas's hand and replied, "We can't stay here, Lucas. Raymond can't see her."

"This might change things, Isabella. He might straighten up for Doris."

"He didn't want her, Lucas," Isabella dryly replied.

"What do you mean?"

"Lucas, he wanted me to terminate her."

As soon as the words slipped out of her mouth, Lucas knew his role of protector was just beginning. Why would Raymond not want the child? Would Raymond try to hurt her? Lucas pushed the thoughts out of his mind and focused on his actions. He turned and asked the midwife if she would hold the baby. "You're going to Irene's house."

Isabella nodded as she lifted her arms for Lucas to carry her to his car. Lucas knew that Irene's house would be safe and that Irene would know how to take care of the child better than he could. He wished with everything that he could care for Isabella and Doris, but knew that taking her to his apartment would be too risky for the both of them.

Lucas walked back into the home and took Doris from the midwife. The woman looked confused, but Lucas had to get the two most important women in his life out of that house before their tormenter returned. He looked at the woman and begged, "Please, don't tell anyone."

The woman put her hand to her mouth and agreed. Lucas was hopeful she would say nothing to Raymond. He touched her shoulder out of gratitude and walked back with Doris in his arms. Rain fell and the April air began to get a little cooler. He handed Doris to her mother. Lucas got in the car and drove away, praying that he would never again have to return to that house.

Lucas arrived at Irene's home and knocked on the door with Doris in his arms. It took a while for Fred to answer, but when he opened the door, Lucas could see the confusion on Fred's face. Fred asked what Lucas was doing there, but Lucas asked to speak to his sister. Irene came to the door and gasped when she saw the small child in a blanket.

"Is this Isabella's baby?" she asked as she reached out for the child.

"Doris," Lucas replied as he handed his sister the infant. He turned to Fred and asked, "Can they stay here?"

"Of course," he replied. He and Lucas walked out through the rain to the car. Fred held a blanket over Isabella as Lucas carried her into their home. Fred led him to the spare room where he placed Isabella on the bed to rest. She was asleep, and Lucas was thankful. He had to tell Irene what happened.

Irene changed Isabella's clothes again and tucked her into the spare bed.

The baby slept in Irene's arms for the rest of the night. The warm fire stove was Lucas's only comfort. He rubbed his eyes, still in shock of all he witnessed. "She was just screaming."

Irene lifted her eyes, "Who?"

Lucas swallowed. "Isabella. She called and she was screaming. I rushed over and saw her laying there, yelling. I called the midwife, but I could not find Raymond. I have no clue where he went."

"Where could he have gone?" Fred asked as he paced back in forth, looking too angry at Raymond to rejoice for the new life in the room.

Lucas replied, "To get more liquor, I assume."

"You have to ask her what happened tomorrow when she wakes up. She trusts you more than any of us."

Lucas nodded his head and asked, "Could I sleep on your sofa tonight?"

Irene and Fred both agreed to let him stay the night, which was less than Lucas could have hoped for. He wished that Isabella could have had a beautiful night filled with happiness and celebration instead of fearful running. Lucas wished better for Isabella and hoped that one day he would have the chance to give that to her and Doris.

Isabella woke up the next morning with a sore stomach, but a smile on her bruised face. She sensed Lucas sitting in the chair next to her bed. He was reading the paper, and everything felt perfectly right. When she rubbed her eyes, her reality hit. She winced in pain. Isabella was sure her eyes were black, just as before. Lucas had come to her rescue again, which was quite embarrassing. She sat up slowly, which got Lucas's attention. "Are you all right?"

Isabella swallowed with a nod. "Where's Doris?"

Lucas smiled, which made Isabella's heart rate ease. "She's with Irene."

"Good." The silence was so thick one could cut it with a letter opener. Isabella reached for the water beside her bed and took a sip. "Thank you, Lucas."

He nodded and smiled, but Isabella knew he was looking for an explanation as to why she called him. Isabella took another drink of water. "He came home drinking again."

"You don't have to tell me if you're not ready," Lucas urged as he sat on the side of the bed and took her hand.

Isabella smiled, wondering why she was so lucky to have a friend like Lucas. "He came home drinking, and one thing led to another, and he kept hitting me, but this time I was too weak to fight him off as quick as last time." She sniffed and tried to keep her emotions intact. She put her hand on her stomach. "He hit her. She decided to fight back. She's a fighter."

Her heart steadied as she held his hand a little tighter. She smiled at Lucas. "Then you got there, and I don't remember a lot of what else happened."

Lucas wiped her tears. Isabella was glad he was tender enough to wipe them. She asked for Doris. Lucas left the room. Isabella stared at the wall in front of her and saw Raymond's angry expression in her mind. A tear fell from her eye, and it was then that she decided that she would no longer cry for Raymond. She was done. Her child deserved better than a man who would come home at night to beat her. Lucas came back with Doris in his arms. Isabella gleamed at her beautiful daughter. As she held her in her arms, tears fell from her eyes on to Doris's small body. "Hi, Doris. It's Momma." Isabella wiped the tears. She looked at Lucas as a tear ran down her cheek. Her eyes grew colder. "This changes everything, Lucas. I don't want him to touch her."

"Then we won't let him."

Chapter 12

"The baby's crying again," Fred shouted to his houseguest. Isabella ran into the bedroom where she slept. Seeing Doris lying there with tears dripping down the side of her face was pitiful. Isabella was sure she could make the tears disappear with a change of diaper or some milk. She picked up her one-month-old and rocked her in her arms. It seemed all Doris needed was her mother's attention. Isabella looked at her daughter's chocolate eyes and small smile. She was incandescently happy. Her child was alive and well, and her own injuries from Raymond's fists were almost healed. Soon, she could show her face in public and flaunt her baby to all of the other mothers in the town. She looked forward to the many different playtimes with her daughter and her daughter's friends. When Irene's child was born, her child and Doris could play daily.

Isabella carried her daughter into the living area. "It looks as if she just missed her mother."

"What a spoiled child," Fred replied as he sipped his morning coffee.

"Just wait until your baby arrives, I'm sure you'll spoil it just the same."

Isabella slowly bounced her child to sleep as she looked out the window before her. She saw the trees had gained back their lost color. Spring was in full swing, but maybe it was the arrival of Doris that brightened the world for Isabella. Nonetheless, she was happy to live in a world where her daughter was the center. If only Raymond would work on his temper. Even so, Isabella was too afraid for Doris to even think about moving back with her husband.

"What a cute little girl," Irene said in a childlike voice.

"Good morning." Isabella smiled.

"How are you feeling today?"

Isabella lowered her voice to let Doris sleep. "Great. I'll be able to run errands with you in a few days."

"We should have a doctor come see you before we do anything too drastic." Irene accepted her husband's kiss as he left for work and then turned her attention back to her friend. "Your face seems to have healed; you can't even tell it was bruised."

With a small smile Isabella replied, "Thank you."

Irene sat on the sofa, and Isabella sat opposite her. She could feel Irene looking at her, but tried to focus on Doris to avoid Irene's questions.

"What did you tell my brother?" Irene asked with her hands to her mouth.

Isabella cleared her throat and looked up at her friend, trying to read into her question. She gave a small smile and replied, "I told him what happened, and I thanked him for helping me. Why?"

Isabella watched as Irene folded her arms across her pink cotton blouse. "You need to talk with him."

She shook her head. "I don't know what you mean."

"Yes, you do," Irene replied, slightly raising her voice. Isabella opened her eyes wider and tilted her head toward Doris to signal to Irene that the baby was sleeping. Irene softly continued, "I've given you passes before, but you have to tell me what's going on between you and Lucas."

Isabella was truly shocked by her accusation and hastily replied, "There's nothing going on between me and Lucas."

Isabella stood and left the room to put Doris back in her bed. Why would Irene bring this up now? It had only been a month after her and Raymond's separation. She knew the argument that was about to take place. Isabella was fully aware that she would have to confront her buried feelings in a matter of seconds. She walked back into the living space and sat back in the chair and commented, "She needs sleep."

"You cannot get out of this conversation, Isabella. I've been waiting for the right time for a while now."

"And this is the right time?"

"I don't think there'll ever be one."

"What do you want me to say?" Isabella asked throwing her hands in the air.

"I want you to tell me how you feel, and I want you to tell me now. Lucas has been through a great deal, and I don't want to see either one of you hurt."

Isabella placed her hands back in her lap and looked at her palms. She stared at her wedding band and replied with deep regret, "I think I love him."

Isabella looked up to see Irene looking back at her. It was as if Irene had seen a ghost. "You think?"

Isabella looked into her best friend's eyes and confessed, "I love him. I love him. I love him…and I think I have for a very long time."

Irene's smile seemed bittersweet as it glided across her lips. "I thought so."

"Why are you asking me this now? Why are you asking me this at all? Even if I love him and he loves me back, I'm married. I'm married, and I have Doris to think about," she replied, trying to keep her tears at bay.

"Exactly. You have to think about Doris. Do you want her to have a father like Raymond?" Irene asked as she tried to reason with Isabella.

Isabella saw what Irene was implying. She was certainly not going to divorce Raymond. The risk was too great. She could lose Doris and be left with nothing. Isabella looked at her friend and replied, "There's too much risk involved."

"We have more rights now, Isabella. We can vote now. They could let you keep Doris. Things are changing!"

"My daughter's life is not a bet. I'll stay with Raymond, but I'll live separately."

Irene raised her voice, "That makes no sense! Then why are you still here with us? It has been a month and you seem fine. I just don't understand."

"Do you want me to leave?"

Irene rolled her eyes, which upset Isabella. "No."

Isabella raised her voice to match Irene's. "Did it ever occur to you that I'm terrified to go home? Do you know what it's like to feel unappreciated and to be humiliated to show your face to the public most of the year because it always has at least one bruise?" Tears began to fall. "Do you know what it's like to have the man who once vowed to love you and care for you, beat you until you get away or he gets too exhausted to keep going? No. Until you feel those things, don't tell me how or when to return to it."

Isabella quickly wiped her tears when she saw Irene's horrific expression of guilt. She walked over to her friend and took her hand, "Irene, I'm doing the best I can. I'm sorry I raised my voice, but you have to understand that I'd leave in a heartbeat if it weren't for the marriage and the promise I made to Raymond. I just cannot do it."

Irene touched her hand, which brought comfort to Isabella. Isabella took a breath and tried to forget about her own troubles. She looked at her friend, and her friend looked back as if all was forgiven. Isabella smiled, and Irene returned the smile with a soft grin. Isabella sniffed and commented, "Now, let's narrow down names for your little one."

Lucas finished his entry and stuffed his journal in his desk drawer. He had not been able to journal in weeks, because his days were busy. Plus, his emotions were too real and too frightening to write down on paper. It was not that he feared writing them down, but that he feared if he wrote them down, they would be permanently bound to reality. Lucas looked out the window and saw the busy streets of New Orleans. The people were going on about their lives as if they were forever satisfied with what little life they led. Lucas smiled, knowing they could never truly be satisfied with this life. He turned when he heard his name called. His boss was looking down on him. "I want an outline of your story on my desk tomorrow morning."

"Does it have to be about the protests again?" Lucas blankly asked.

"Give me something new," the old fat man replied as he stroked his dark beard. Lucas nodded and agreed to find something new and refreshing. Lucas had no clue where to begin. He sat at his desk for hours, waiting for an idea to come to him, but one never came. He looked at the small pictures on his desk and saw a picture of Irene, Isabella, and himself. It was his favorite. Irene and Isabella were about twelve, and he was about sixteen years old. The year was 1910, almost fifteen years ago. He already knew then that he would one day marry Isabella. He looked at the writing on the back of the photo and saw messy letters relaying the message, "Friends always, now and forever." Lucas shoved his paper and pens into his small drawer and looked at the picture. He needed to see Isabella. Maybe if he saw her, inspiration would come, as it always had. He packed up, said good-bye to his fellow workers, and headed to Irene's home.

Isabella's heart skipped a beat when she saw Lucas on the other side of the door. It was as if she was meeting him for the first time. She gave a polite smile as she opened the door and asked, "Lucas, what's wrong?"

"Nothing. I just came to see how you and Doris were doing."

Isabella looked at him closely and could tell there was something different about him. It was almost as if they were both young again. Isabella let him inside, and they both joined Irene in the kitchen. Isabella glanced at Irene, who gave her a reassuring look that everything would be okay. Isabella waited by the cucumbers as Irene and Lucas spoke with one another. She looked at the back of his head and then to Irene's slightly wrinkled face. Isabella wondered when they had gotten so old. Not that any age below seventy was old, but that they were no longer in their twenties. Isabella smiled when she thought back on the wonderful times they had growing up together. Irene was like her sister in every way, and Lucas was, well, Lucas.

"Is that all right with you?"

Isabella heard these words and snapped her head toward her friends. "I'm sorry."

Irene smiled as she wiped her hands. "I need more flour from down the street. Lucas is going to go with me. Is that all right?"

Isabella looked at Lucas, whose lips were pressed tightly together. That meant he wanted to speak with her alone. She could recognize that anywhere. "I can go with Lucas and take Doris out. She and I could use the fresh air."

"Are you all right to do that?" Irene asked in a timid voice. Isabella knew it was brought on by her brother's presence and not the simple fact of her going out.

Isabella smiled and gave Irene an affirmative nod, "I'll go get Doris."

Lucas watched as Isabella rounded the corner with her child in her arms. It was a sight that brought warmth to him, something he had not felt since last seeing Isabella. He opened the door for her and waved good-bye to his sister. It was obvious how much Irene knew about his and Isabella's friendship. Lucas only wished that she had not spilled the news of his affection to Isabella.

Isabella put Doris in a carriage that was once Lucas's. It was a perfect sight. If only he could purchase a new carriage for Isabella and Doris. The thing they were using was almost thirty years old. They walked for a while, and Doris slept. Surprisingly, they made it to town in no time at all, and with no more than a conversation about the weather. Lucas was surprised at just how close they lived to town. He looked over at Isabella and asked, "How are you?"

"I'm doing well."

"And Doris?"

"Perfect, except at night. The child won't close her eyes."

"You shouldn't let her sleep during the day," Lucas suggested as his eyes lit up.

Silence was all Lucas heard for a while. Isabella stayed quiet, which made the walk all the more strange for Lucas. As they came closer to the central part of town, Lucas turned to Isabella and commented, "I miss you, Isabella." She looked at him with a raised eyebrow, in which time he immediately regretted saying anything. He looked at Doris and then to Isabella. "I mean that I never see you as often as I used to."

"With a baby and no home, there's really no time for me to come visit."

Lucas smiled, as he replied, "No, I by no means blame you I'd like to visit more, if that's all right with you. I just want to be a part of Doris's life and yours."

Isabella looked at Doris and then back to him. "Very well."

Lucas looked in the distance and saw his office a few stores down. He was hit with the memory of the photograph he found earlier that day. He knew Isabella would love the old picture and her ancient feeble handwriting. "I need to fetch something from the office. Do you want to come?"

Isabella looked at Doris's peaceful slumber and with a wave of her hand in front of her nose, she replied, "She's asleep, and I need to change her. I'll be fine."

Lucas felt odd leaving Isabella and Doris alone on their first outing since the night of Doris's arrival. Although he was reluctant, Lucas vowed to be back within seconds.

Isabella smelled the ugly odor coming from her child. She looked both ways before entering a small open space between shops. It was not very polite to change your child in the middle of the street, or at least Isabella thought that much. She searched for a clean cloth and changed her baby. Isabella tickled her feet and played with Doris once she woke up. It was curious to Isabella how much Lucas was interested in her and Doris, but it was also very comforting to know that someone was watching over them.

"There you are," a familiar voice called from behind.

Isabella turned to see her husband staring her straight in the face with a brown bag in his scarred hands. Her heart stopped. This had to be a dream. She held her breath. Isabella grasped the sides of the baby carriage and prayed that God would save her and her child from him. He approached her, and with one swing, he threw her away from her baby and into the wall. Isabella stood up, refusing to leave without Doris safe in her arms.

"So you went ahead and had it, and with Lucas by your side."

She looked into his lifeless eyes. "Raymond, put her down!"

"I told you I didn't want her," he said as he forcefully dropped Doris into her carriage.

"You don't have to keep her, Raymond. I can keep her," Isabella reasoned with her hands up, ready to defend herself.

"With him?" Raymond rolled his eyes and took a stab at her, which she avoided. Isabella prayed Lucas would come back soon. Raymond swung again and hit her on the side of her head. Isabella hit the ground with a stiff *thud* and was only awake long enough to see Raymond going after Doris with his fist ready and his anger overflowing.

Lucas walked back to the store and could not see Isabella anywhere. He searched and asked policemen for help to find her, worried. Lucas checked the small opening between two of the shops and saw a crazed man beating Doris's carriage. He immediately identified the man as Raymond Dailey and yelled for the police. He saw Isabella laying on the ground. He tackled Raymond from behind, freeing Doris of his fists. Lucas beat him as if tomorrow would never come. When the police arrived, they apprehended Raymond and called for medical care for baby Doris and Isabella.

The world was spinning when Lucas picked up a frightfully silent Doris. He held her and walked over to Isabella, hoping the sight of her mother would get her crying. Lucas noticed that Doris's eyes were shut. She was breathing too slow. "We need medical help now!" Lucas yelled. He slowly rocked Doris, pleading for her to open her eyes.

Lucas looked at Isabella, who was unconscious. He was angry and confused, trying to figure out what had happened and why it had taken place. There had to be a reason, but Lucas could not see it. He did not want to see it. All he wanted was for Doris to open her eyes and for Isabella to get the chance to hold her baby one more time.

The medical service arrived and got both Doris and Isabella into the car to transport them to a hospital. Lucas held Doris's hand with one hand and Isabella's hand with his other as they drove to the hospital. A man hit Doris's chest, which made her cry. Lucas was never happier to hear a baby cry. The people and places were a blur. Time had stopped the moment he had seen Raymond. Lucas held Isabella's hand tight, blaming himself for leaving her alone. This was his fault.

When they arrived, the nurses took Doris out of his arms and into a backroom. Isabella was placed on a bed, and they waited for her to wake up. Lucas paced back and forth in front of the bed, not knowing what to do with himself. Finally, he pulled up a chair and sat next to Isabella, holding her hand as if the fact that he loved her would jolt her awake. He watched the people in the room as they roamed about doing their jobs. The clock was taunting him. He figured Irene was wondering where they were. Lucas had never wanted to make this phone call, although, he always had the feeling he would do so one day. Today was *one day*. He walked over to the phone and dialed Irene's home.

Chapter 13

Lucas greeted a frantic Irene at the entrance of the hospital. He could see the guilt in her eyes as she hung on to her husband. When she saw Lucas, she let go of Fred. Lucas embraced her, wishing there was more he could do for them. He held his sister as she sobbed. Lucas's green eyes leaked as he heard Irene's concerned whimper. Lucas drew back and informed Irene and Fred, "Isabella's breathing, and they believe she'll wake up soon. Maybe a concussion." He wiped his face to rid it of tears. "Doris is in worse condition, and they're doing tests on her now."

"How can we help?" Fred asked as he put his hands on his wife's shoulders.

Lucas glanced at his pregnant sister and replied, "Nothing but keep calm, I'm afraid."

He sat with Fred as Irene went to see Isabella alone. Lucas felt as if he was in a nightmare. He wished he was. He prayed that they would both recover. Knowing that this was the closest Raymond had ever come to taking both Doris and Isabella's lives, there was no way Isabella would go back to him. Lucas was glad for it, because he hated seeing the woman he loved being treated so poorly. He detested seeing Raymond even looking at Doris. The thought of it infuriated him. Irene came out of the room crying and stated that she never wanted to see Isabella like that again. It was bad enough before, but this time Raymond had gone too far. Lucas agreed.

Lucas rubbed his hands together as he walked back to Isabella's bed. There was a curtain separating them from the other patients, so, not much in the way of privacy. He looked at her black hair and her peaceful features. It was as if she was in the middle of a heavenly dream. Lucas prayed she would not wake up to her greatest nightmare. He pondered why this happened to Isabella. She had been through so much already, and the fact that Raymond had hardened her heart made Lucas all the more terrified for her soul when she awoke. The doctor interrupted Lucas's thoughts when he drew back the curtain. The man seemed professional, but he also had a weary kindness about him. It looked as if the man had been crying. Lucas called Irene and Fred over to hear the update on Doris.

The kind man asked them all to sit as he sat his clipboard down. Lucas knew the news before it even came out of the man's wrinkled mouth. He clenched Isabella's hand, hoping that she could not hear the conversation that was about to unfold.

"We did everything we could…"

Lucas could not bear to hear anything else the doctor had to say. He did not want to know how or why Doris died; all he wanted was to strangle Raymond Dailey for murdering the one bright light on planet Earth. Lucas looked at the doctor when he asked, "Are you the father?"

Lucas's heart was breaking, but those words cut to the bone. He looked at the man and shook his head, but knew in his heart that he was more of a father to Doris than Raymond had ever thought of being. It made him sick. Irene stood up and left, too shocked to even comprehend the news. Fred followed her, but Lucas sat and listened. He listened to Isabella's heartbeat, and he listened to her breathing. He waited for an answer as to why it all happened.

Lucas did not leave Isabella's side until the next morning. The police came to question him. Lucas had not slept much that pervious night, in hopes that Isabella would wake up. He was pulled into a room with a policeman and blankly gave his witness statement. He was in a daze, numb to his feelings, and blinded by the scene he had witnessed.

"Was this the first account?"

Lucas slowly pushed back his chair. "No, sir, but first with the child."

"Why did he attack?"

Lucas looked at the man, swallowed, and then replied, "They're staying with my sister. She's outside. Talk to her."

The policeman nodded and let Lucas out of the room. He felt a tingle in his nose. Lucas walked back with a nurse to Isabella's new room. The nurse informed him that she would need to be cleared by a doctor after hearing the news of her daughter's death before she could leave. Lucas reached for her hand as the nurse continued to read off her different vitals, or at least he assumed that was what she was reading off to him. Lucas kept his eyes on Isabella. After the nurse finally left the room, Lucas sat next to her bed—a sight too familiar for him. If only he had stayed with them. What was that picture worth anyways? Nothing, yet it cost Isabella everything.

Three hours later, Lucas resorted to reading the week-old newspaper left in the room by the previous occupant. He began to read, but quickly drifted to sleep.

Isabella opened her eyes and felt pressure in her head and pain in her arm. She blinked to clear her vision and stared at the white ceiling above her. She knew she was in a bed, and the white room and beeping machines gave her the clue she was in a hospital. Isabella tried to put the pieces together and looked to her left. Lucas was asleep. Her heart rate rose when she could not see Doris anywhere in the room. Lucas woke up to the beeping machines and rushed to her side. Isabella was terrified, but felt somewhat comfortable looking at Lucas and knowing he was with her. He brushed her hair out of her eyes and knelt by her bed. Lucas rubbed her hand, which was something that always made her weak in the stomach. Isabella closed her eyes. "What happened?"

Lucas leaned in closer. "It was Raymond. He fractured your arm and gave you a bad concussion. They want to watch you overnight again and then you can go home, but before that they need to clear you."

Isabella licked her lips and swallowed. Lucas got her a glass of water and returned to her side. Isabella sipped slowly and then looked back at Lucas. He seemed too distant for that to be the only news he had to deliver. "Where's Doris?"

Lucas opened his mouth and tears started to pour from his eyes. He did not have to say a word for Isabella to know what he was going to say. She stared at him as he dryly replied, "They did everything they could."

Isabella's lips quivered as she tried to smile. She blinked and shook her head, not wanting to believe that the monster she married killed their child with his own hands. Her precious baby. Isabella broke down and cried. A part of her died as she gasped for air, trying to comprehend her situation. Lucas embraced her, which eased a small portion of her extensive amount of anguish and utter torment. She cried until her tears would no longer come. Lucas cried with her, holding her and supporting her. Right now they needed each other, and Isabella's heart sunk further when she realized that they always had.

The next day, the police visited Isabella. It was intimidating and surreal to see the police asking if she was ready to talk.

Isabella felt like she would never be ready to talk. Lucas squeezed her hand and replied for her, "Not now."

Isabella looked at Lucas, grateful that he was trying to protect her. Before the police turned to leave, she said, "I'll talk with you as best as I can."

"He has to leave the room," one of the policemen said, pointing to Lucas.

Isabella nodded and turned to Lucas. "I can do it."

"I'll be just outside the door."

As Lucas waited, all he could think about was seeing Isabella lying on the cobblestone street, unconscious. He tried to erase the memory and replace it with a brighter one. His mind was incapable of eradicating the blame he placed on himself. If he had spoken up sooner, Isabella would be his wife and none of this would have happened. If only he had forced Isabella to leave her husband, Doris would still be alive. If only he had not left them alone for those brief seconds. Lucas could tire himself out with "if only." What mattered was what happened and how he could help Isabella through her grief.

Lucas looked to his right as his sister joined him. Irene laid her head on his arm and commented, "It's my fault." Lucas was burnt by her words.

"No one is at fault but Raymond." Irene shook her head. "I knew what he was like, or at least I had a feeling. I just wanted her to be happy. She was so hurt over…" Irene looked at her brother as if she had told a valuable secret.

Lucas squinted and asked, "What?"

"Never mind," Irene replied as she gently dabbed her nose.

Lucas wondered what Irene wanted to keep from him, but he immediately forgot about it when the policemen exited the room. He shook hands with the officers and thanked them for their service.

"You won't have to worry about Mr. Dailey again. He'll be incarcerated for the rest of his life, I'll make sure of it."

Lucas gave them what little smile he had left to give. He motioned for Irene to go into the room. "I'll let you two be alone."

He pushed his hands into his pockets and headed toward the waiting area. The pale painting in the waiting room was taunting. Seeing a beautiful depiction of a beach was not too comforting for grieving persons. What was the purpose of these rooms other than a place to cry alone? Doris was gone. It was an empty feeling that he knew would take years to heal. Lucas Matthews ached for Isabella and the excruciating pain she was bound to feel. He closed his sore eyes tightly, as if closing his eyes would erase the problems at hand.

Isabella wiped her eyes when Irene entered the room. She was glad to see her closest friend, but not glad to be with company all day. Irene sat next to Isabella, and that was all it took for Isabella to completely lose control of her emotions. When her eyes met Irene's they began to leak tears. This leakage turned into an ocean of tears from both women. Isabella could not breathe, but somehow she was able to keep living through the torture. She took Irene's hand and grasped it tightly, holding on to the little sanity she had left. Isabella's throat burned as she gasped for air. Irene took Isabella's face in her hands, and the two breathed deeply together. After Isabella was finished, she wiped her face with her blanket. "I don't understand."

Irene gave a bitter smile. "Sometimes we're not meant to understand. God works in mysterious ways."

Isabella looked at the ground and saw her daughter's face in her mind. She sniffed and replied, "I hate him, Irene. I hate him so much."

"Raymond?"

Isabella kept her eyes focused on the ground. "No, I hate God."

Chapter 14

Three months later, Lucas helped Isabella to a chair in the living area of Irene's home. She was distant, which was expected. However, Lucas knew that she was strong and capable of understanding that there was a bigger picture unfolding for her. It was easy for him to say, because he was not the one whose daughter was murdered. He sat across from Isabella and asked if she wanted anything. Pointing to the baby toys all over the living area, she slowly shook her head. Lucas nodded and picked up the toys, which he assumed he would store in a box so that Isabella could look through them when the time came for her to move out of Irene's house.

He wanted to take her pain and relocate it into his own body. Isabella had lost her parents, her husband, and her child. She had no one left but Lucas and Irene. He bent down and offered, "Water?"

Isabella replied with a feeble head nod that was barely clear enough to see. She had not spoken a word since she had declared her hate for God. This fact scared Lucas to death.

Irene came into the kitchen with groceries. She placed them on the counter and then looked at Lucas with wide eyes. His sister was about to have her child, and Isabella was not ready to witness that. Lucas knew he would never be ready to witness that. He rolled his eyes, frustrated that the baby would choose to come so soon. Irene shook her head and talked to her baby. "Not here, not now. This can't be happening."

Lucas dropped the glass of water and took his sister's hands, hoping Fred could take over and he could distract Isabella long enough for the baby to be delivered. Thankfully, Fred came into the home soon after. Lucas passed his sister to him as if she was a hot skillet. He walked into the living area, attempting to keep calm. He opened the backdoor and gestured toward the outdoors. Isabella looked at him and shook her head. He rolled his eyes knowing that if she did not leave, Irene would end up having to have her baby in the kitchen. Lucas looked at the idle Isabella and grew angry. He walked over to her and looked at her in the eyes until she was forced into making eye contact with him. Lucas took her hand gently and ushered her out the doors. Fred and Irene frantically made their way into the bathroom.

As Lucas closed the doors behind them, he looked at Isabella, who quickly sat on the porch. Lucas took a breath. "Is it going to be like this?"

Isabella gave no response. Lucas sat next to her and looked at the perfectly blue August sky. "It's okay to be sad, but this isn't okay."

She gave him a sour look, but Lucas continued, "We can sit here all day if we need to, Isabella."

Isabella crossed her arms around her stomach and looked away from him.

"It isn't okay to stop living."

This got Isabella's attention. She turned to look at him as he continued, "We couldn't save her. We failed. We grieve. We move on. We remember her."

Isabella stood up and walked away with a look of disgust for what Lucas was saying. Lucas followed her. He caught up to her and spoke to her back. "I'm sorry, okay? I'm sorry I couldn't save her, but that wasn't up to me." Isabella hurried her pace, but Lucas was determined to get through to her. Lucas raised his voice as he came to an epiphany of his own. "You owe her more than this!"

Isabella turned to face him with tears in her eyes. She stared at him for what seemed like an eternity. "What, Lucas, what do I owe her?"

Lucas approached her slowly. "She would want you to live. Not just to live, but to love. To love living."

"How can I love life if she's not in it?"

Lucas walked closer, carefully suggesting, "Because *the one* who loves you the most gave it to you to live for him."

Isabella wiped her tears and folded her hands across her chest. "What if this is it?"

"What do you mean?"

"What if I get dead parents, an abusive husband, and a dead baby. Lucas, what if that's it for me?"

"That is not all there is for you."

"How could you possibly know that?" Isabella looked at the man she loved and saw the pity in his eyes. It disgusted her. It all started with him, and it all would end with him. Isabella shook her head and commented, "Seven years, Lucas. Seven years."

Isabella could not stand to look at him anymore and turned to go, hoping he would not follow her.

"What does that mean, Isabella?"

Isabella turned and faced him. "My parents died and you stopped talking to me. Seven years it took for me to move on. Then Raymond, he was so kind. Doris was the best thing I've ever done, and he took her away." She began to cry. "He took them all away, Lucas. God took it all! Why?"

She fell into him and he held her. She tried to piece together God's puzzle without all the pieces.

Lucas held Isabella and waited for her to stop crying. It was a good thing, the tears, because at least he now knew she was feeling something. When she gathered herself, she drew back and apologized, but Lucas reminded her that she had nothing for which to apologize. He took her by the shoulders and looked into her chocolate eyes. "I'll always be here for you."

"I've been alone for so long…"

"You'll always have me."

She nodded slowly and took his arm as they walked back toward the home. The sun was hot, but it seemed brighter that day.

As they opened the doors and walked back into the house, they were greeted by Irene lying in the living area with a baby in her arms. Isabella opened her mouth and gave her dear friend a wide smile, something she had not done in a long time. Isabella looked back to Lucas and smiled, assuming he knew about the baby and wanted to prepare her before meeting the new addition. Isabella sat next to Irene and looked at the precious face of Irene's little girl. Irene passed her to Isabella as she announced, "Meet Margaret Doris Hartley."

Isabella looked at Irene, and the two held each other's hands tightly, signifying an unbreakable bond. Isabella knew that with the help of her remarkable friends, she could learn to love life again, starting with little Margaret.

A Year Later

"Could you pass me a bowl?" Isabella asked as she stuck a spoon into the vat of ice cream.

Lucas slid her two bowls. She scooped the delicious treat out of its container and into the bowls. Isabella smiled as Irene and Fred waved good-bye, worried sick to leave their precious Margaret alone with Lucas and Isabella. Isabella assured her that all would be fine, but new mothers rarely ponder things going right. As the door shut, Lucas left the room to tend to a crying Margaret. Isabella was thankful Lucas offered to help her care for Margaret. She was still not keen on being alone, so Lucas's presence made the night all the more relaxing. Isabella brought the bowls into the living area and gave one to her friend. Lucas placed Margaret on a blanket, and the two watched her every move. After the ice cream was finished and the bowls were washed, Lucas commented, "Why did they have to go to the dinner?"

Isabella smiled as she rounded the corner. "It was for Fred's promotion."

"Guest of honor," Lucas sarcastically replied with a shake of his hands.

"They needed to get out of the house," Isabella stated as she took a seat next to Lucas.

Lucas gave a small smirk. Isabella looked at her friend and rolled her eyes, but Lucas defended himself. "You haven't left the house in almost a year."

Isabella gave him an eye roll, slightly offended by his lack of empathy. She squinted her eyes and asked, "Why do you think that is?"

Isabella saw the realization flicker in Lucas's eyes, as he replied, "I was just…"

She took a breath. "I can't leave here without thinking of her. Like you said, it has almost been a year now."

Lucas looked at Isabella's hard expression and picked up Margaret, as if looking at the child would make the night less cumbersome. Margaret brought life into the dull and anger-filled room, but Lucas held on to the hope that Isabella could one day let go of her anger. She was trying to, he could tell by the way she was acting. She needed further healing. His face brought back memories of the worst night of her life, and Lucas knew that leaving her alone after tonight would be better for them both. He rubbed his eyes and came to the realization that she needed to heal separately from him.

"I used to tell myself 'If only I could've fought him off or left earlier'."

"You can't blame yourself, Isabella."

"I know that now. I'm just so frustrated with myself. How could I have not seen it sooner?"

"It was God's plan."

"What a lovely plan it was," she said rolling her eyes. She stood to go.

"Where are you going?"

"I need to go to sleep. Can you put her down?"

"Isabella, don't blame yourself or God. Blame him."

Isabella looked back at Lucas with tired eyes. "Can you put her down?"

"Sure," Lucas replied as she retreated into her room. Lucas looked at Margaret and gave a sigh. He knew he had to leave the next morning; it was what was best for them all.

The next day, Lucas put his things into the back of his trunk, much to his sister's dismay. He tried to block out her nagging voice as he threw his last shirt into his car. He turned to see his sister with the baby in her arms and a frown on her face. "Cheer up, Irene, I just need space."

"Space from what?"

"Space, that's all," Lucas replied as he looked through the window to Isabella. She was staring at him as if she knew he was leaving because of her. Lucas waved to the window, but Isabella did not smile back. He kissed his niece good-bye. He looked back at Isabella and commented, "She needs it too."

With an understanding sigh, Irene let him go in peace. Lucas was happy that his sister cared for Isabella, but was not too happy that she still had hopes he and she would be good friends again. Lucas rolled his eyes as he turned away from his sister's hopeful features. It was idiotic to think that he and Isabella could fully restore their friendship. He prayed Isabella would soon come to find happiness not only in herself, but in the one who created her. That was Isabella's problem, she did not trust in him.

It was all Raymond's fault. What had provoked him to harm baby Doris? As Lucas drove back to his apartment, he could not rid the pull to confront Raymond once and for all. He did not need an explanation or an apology. He needed to see that Raymond was suffering. Before Lucas knew it, he was turning toward prison and away from his residence. He had to see Raymond. Maybe if he saw Isabella's tormenter, he could make more sense of the situation.

Lucas pulled up to the facility an hour later. He entered the prison and asked to see Raymond Dailey. They laughed at him and called Raymond from his cell. It took half an hour for Raymond to appear behind the bars. Lucas's blood was frozen. Raymond was unrecognizable. His nose had been broken over five times, and the rest of his body was either bruised or cut. Raymond spoke first. "Why are you here, Lucas?"

Lucas swallowed. "I came to see you."

"Why?"

"I wanted to see you."

"Well, here I am."

Lucas awaited an apology. He cleared his throat and commented, "I take it you are not finding friends here."

Raymond laughed and replied, "No."

There was a pause, and Lucas grew even more uncomfortable. He was about to leave when Raymond continued, "I hope she is doing well. I regret it every day. I hope you know that."

Lucas listened closely, and Raymond explained, "I was a jealous drunk. I know I don't deserve it, but I hope one day you could forgive me for what I have done. I've done so much harm, I know, but I hope you believe me when I say how truly sorry I am."

Lucas looked into Raymond's broken eyes. He did not know how to feel. The man before him killed Doris and beat Isabella. He destroyed countless lives. Lucas wanted with everything that he was to spit in his face, but something unexplainable overcame Lucas as he stared at Raymond. Lucas sniffed. "Isabella may not feel the same, but I forgive you, Raymond. Not because I think what you did was excusable by any means. I forgive you because I have been forgiven."

Raymond's eyes filled with water as he pleaded, "Please, I do not deserve any kind of forgiveness."

Lucas replied, "No one earns forgiveness, Raymond. Forgiveness is given. I forgive you."

Raymond shook his head in disbelief as Lucas stood to leave. It took everything in Lucas to remain calm. He could never condone or defend what Raymond did. However, as Lucas walked out to his vehicle, there was an overwhelming peace about him.

After driving a while, Lucas pulled up to his apartment and unloaded his things, thankful that he still had things to unload. A newspaper was at his feet, stating that the Red Sox had beaten the Yankees, but Lucas was not in the mood to care. He walked up to his apartment, a place he had not stepped foot in since Doris's death, almost a year ago. He closed his eyes, grabbed the knob, and opened his door to a new future.

Chapter 15

A Year Later

I rene was such a wonderful mother, like Isabella knew she would have been. It was almost comical how good Irene was with Margaret. It had been years since Isabella had truly laughed, but she felt like herself again. Little Margaret was almost two years old, which would soon mark exactly two and a half years without Doris. Time moved so quickly, yet for Isabella each moment without Doris seemed like a lifetime. She knew that Doris would always be with her. All of her would always regret choosing Raymond. She came to realize that what was done was done and there was no use in dwelling on it, like Lucas said the day Margaret was born.

Lucas had not been over in months, which was somewhat frustrating for Isabella. He had been with her almost every day, and now he seemed to have moved on. It was understandable. Isabella knew she could not consume his life forever, but part of her wanted to spend the rest of her days with him by her side. Isabella laughed as she came into the kitchen. She was dressed for Easter Sunday. April was such a beautiful time of year, and it was a perfect day for a picnic at the church.

Church was the usual Easter message, and for Isabella, it was her favorite next to Christmas. She put on her cream hat and walked outside the church to meet Irene and Fred at the bottom of the stairs. Margaret was dressed in a light pink dress that matched her mother's. Isabella wore her pale blue dress that was made of cotton. It was a tradition Isabella was sure to uphold every year. They walked over to their family blanket where Margaret was able to roam about freely. Isabella watched the child as Irene and Fred talked with old women who were desperate for attention. She was chasing Margaret when a man caught her eye in the distance. He was tall and handsome, wearing a new gray suit. There was a pretty woman on his arm. She looked quite dainty and pathetic, but Isabella kept that comment to herself. As the figure came closer, she saw that it was Lucas. Isabella turned to Irene. "Who's that with Lucas over there?"

Irene put her hands to her eyes and replied, "I can't say I've ever seen her."

Isabella was even more irked when she found out from an elderly woman it was Lucas's new woman, Shirley.

Isabella tapped Irene on the shoulder, suggesting they go meet the woman who was draped on Lucas's arm like a sick puppy dog. Irene agreed with a nod of her head and took Isabella's arm in her own.

"I don't think this will do any good."

"I just want to meet her," Isabella said with a plastered grin on her face.

"Very well," Irene commented under her breath.

As they approached, Lucas turned red, which Isabella thought was quite hilarious. He introduced his lady. "Irene, this is Shirley, my date. Shirley, this is Irene, my sister."

"Pleasure."

The snob of a woman turned to Isabella with a cold eye and asked, "Who are you?"

Isabella saw her threatened tone as pitiful. "A friend."

Isabella bit her tongue as Lucas, and the two other women exchanged their pleasantries. She felt Lucas's eyes on her, which was quite irritating. After she and Irene left the two alone, they both decided in an instant that they did not like the woman for Lucas, or at all for that matter.

"She's just so needy," Isabella suggested as they sat down on their picnic blanket.

"I agree," Irene said as she took her baby from an older lady. Fred turned to Isabella and asked, "Who's needy?"

Isabella gave a snarl and tossed her eyes in Lucas's direction. Fred laughed, which made Isabella uncomfortable. "I'm going to meet this woman for myself."

He did just that and was so captivated by her and Lucas that he spent the remainder of the picnic talking with them.

"I just don't understand men," Irene said as she tossed a grape in her mouth.

Isabella looked at Lucas and felt a tug toward him, but kept her distance. His eyes met hers as she replied, "Me either."

The Fourth of July came, and the women were glad to be home and away from the noise.

"I saw Lucas with that Shirley girl the other day," Irene commented, almost reading Isabella's mind.

Isabella dried a plate and then casually replied, "They seem good together."

Irene bounced Margaret on her hip. "I don't like her."

Isabella splashed water on her friend. "Baloney!"

Irene gave a laugh and a snort as she placed Margaret on the floor to play with her dolls. Irene joined Isabella at the sink. "You like her?"

"She's the bee's knees. I don't know why they're not married yet," Isabella said with a bucket of sarcasm.

Isabella was glad to get a laugh out of Irene. She kept on, "Big cheese, that's what she is. Very important."

Irene laughed. "I assume you're not serious."

Isabella dried the last plate and laughed. "What gave it away?"

"Just the fact that you still love him is all." Irene then realized what she blurted out and covered her mouth. She looked apologetically at her friend, "I'm sorry...I."

"My dogs are tired, I'm going to go sit down," Isabella replied, not really knowing what to say to her friend. He was with another woman, and it was not her place to ask anything of him. Isabella sat on the couch and put her head in her hands and laughed at herself. She could think of no better response.

Irene rounded the corner and exclaimed, "Don't cry!"

Isabella lifted her head and revealed to Irene that she was laughing. Isabella waved her hand and said, "I'm sorry, I don't know why that's so funny."

Irene sat next to her friend and softly demanded, "Level with me, Isabella."

Isabella stopped laughing and shrugged her shoulders. "Either way it doesn't matter. We've had this conversation before."

Irene looked at her friend and knew for a fact that if Lucas was hearing their conversation, he would ask her to marry him in a second. "Why do you say that it won't matter?"

Isabella was suspicious of Irene. "He's with someone, and I'm sure he's over what we had all those years ago. He would've said something by now, I'm sure."

Irene's heart leaped for joy, but she kept her excitement contained. "Don't be."

Isabella held her breath. "What are you suggesting?"

Irene shook her head. "Something my brother told me at your engagement."

"My engagement?" Isabella asked, confused.

Irene looked to the ceiling to remember the exact words he said. "He said he couldn't get over you."

"He's probably just being dramatic. You know Lucas."

Irene looked at Isabella and shook her head. "He meant it."

Isabella shook her head and let out a sigh. "Either way, it does not matter. That was years ago! Now, let's tend to dinner before Fred gets home."

Irene looked a little dazed. "Very well, get started. I need more flour at the store. I'll be back soon."

Isabella nodded and left Irene in the living area, suspicious of where she was going and what she was going to do. Surely she was not going to see Lucas, but knowing Irene that was where she was headed. Before Isabella could remind her not to say anything to Lucas, Irene was out the door. Isabella had a sinking feeling that her deepest secret was about to be exposed.

Chapter 16

Irene burst through the apartment door as Lucas took a bite out of his toast. He looked at his sister and lightheartedly commented, "Okay, I'll put it on a plate."

Irene came in and walked up to him which he knew was a bad sign. She had the look in her eyes. The very special look Irene would always give right before she exploded into a rant. Lucas finished his toast and wiped his hands together. "Why are you here?"

"Why are you eating toast for supper?"

Lucas looked at his sister, confused, wondering what his meal had to do with her. His sister reverted back to her pre-explosive expression and asked, "Do you love Shirley?"

"We've been together a month, Irene." Lucas was afraid where this was going. He shook his head and continued, "I don't know her well. She's kind."

"Break it off."

Lucas walked into his kitchen, perplexed as to why his sister was showing up this late begging him to break it off with Shirley. His only guess was Isabella, but he was certainly not going to go there. She was in no place to have her emotions toiled with. He knew very well he would marry her tomorrow if she felt the same as he. That was the point of it, she did not feel the same, and even if she did, she still seemed to resent God. Much to his dismay, Irene walked into the kitchen with hands on her hips. "Are you going to be this stubborn?"

Lucas rolled his eyes. "She doesn't feel the same. I assume she never did."

He turned back around to clean the dishes in the sink, hoping Irene would go back home. Lucas felt a thump on his head and turned to his sister, who had a frustrated tone in her now high-pitched voice.

"It's now or never. That's all I'm saying."

Lucas snapped his head toward her. "Did she say something?"

"What do you think?"

Lucas took a short breath. "It can't be true."

"Just talk with her, Lucas. What do you have to lose?"

Lucas followed his sister to the door, not able to respond before she left. He rubbed his now-aching head and paced around the room. Maybe walking would help him think. It was unclear as to why Irene even came to confess this news after all these years. Did this mean she thought Isabella felt the same, or did this mean she knew Isabella felt the same and was ready? After an hour of these questions circulating in his mind, Lucas came to the conclusion that all women were perplexing and that it would be best if he slept on this news.

Lucas walked into his room, sat on his bed, pulled out his journal, and began to write. Unknown to him, a picture fell out of the journal and under his bed. He wrote about his sister's strange behavior and how exactly he should tell Isabella that he still loved her after all this time. It was no simple task, even if he had nothing to lose. That *nothing* came with Isabella's friendship attached to it, making the *nothing* worth more than anything.

The next morning, Lucas rolled out of bed with the same clothes on he had worn the day before. By her request, he was meeting Shirley for brunch. Lucas hated brunch, because it was as indecisive as him.

He sat across the table from Shirley and quickly stated, "You're great, Shirley, really, but I don't think things are going to work between us."

The woman before him cried as if she had a limb amputated. He rolled his eyes, wondering what he was even doing with her in the first place. He tried to console her, but touching her made the dramatic fit worse. After she finished her wailing, she asked with a sniffled nose, "Is there anyone else?"

Lucas thought about lying, but instead replied, "Yes, I'm afraid…"

His confession was interrupted with another set of loud cries to which he replied, "Very well. Good day."

He left money on the table to pay for their drinks. As he left the tearoom, he asked another man in a similar situation as himself, "What's a brunch anyway? Breakfast or lunch, make up your mind."

The two men stared at each other for a moment and uttered, "Lunch." They left the building and their wailing women. Lucas parted ways with the man and then realized that he would now have to gain the courage to talk to Isabella.

A Year Later

Thanksgiving was strange for Isabella. It had now been three years since Doris's passing, and each day got better. It was as if she was alive again, and her years with Raymond were only a memory. Doris, of course, was with her every moment, but less and less so as time moved forward. Thanksgiving was one of Isabella's favorite holidays; the warmth and lights, outdoors, family and friends, everything was picturesque. Lucas was acting very strange around Isabella. In fact, since he had broken things off with Shirley, his mannerisms had changed. Isabella did not want to analyze them and did not want to concern herself with childish wishes. Margaret hobbled toward Isabella, and she stretched her arms out to catch the little one. It was comforting to hold a child, and either way, Isabella was in love with Irene's family so much so that she was viewed as an aunt. Irene called out to Isabella, "Could you take Margaret inside?"

Isabella nodded and picked up a fussy Margaret.

"What's wrong, little one?" she asked the child as they entered the home. Isabella laid her down to sleep. She turned off the lights and quietly closed the door. She turned around to head back outside and ran straight into the side of a man. "Pardon me."

Isabella's stomach fluttered when Lucas looked at her. "No need to worry."

Isabella walked behind him until they reached the living area. She looked at him and politely asked, "How are you?"

Lucas glanced at her with a hint of speculation in his eyes. "You first."

Isabella blushed slightly as she placed her hands on the back of the sofa. "Good. Margaret's adorable. I spend all the time I can helping Irene."

"Sounds like a good time."

"It has been." Isabella looked outside as the pause in the conversation began to linger. She played with the tassels on her dress, which was a nervous habit. Lucas looked at her, but she kept looking away, fearing that if she looked at him she would say something she should keep to herself.

"Do you regret it?" Lucas asked as he kept his eyes on Isabella.

Isabella felt as if this question was more a test than anything. "No."

Lucas slapped the couch gently with his hands. "Good."

He began to walk away, but Isabella stopped him and asked, "Are you upset with me for some reason?" Lucas tilted his head as if he did not understand her. "I mean, you're acting strange. You've been acting strange for about a year now."

Lucas gave her a smile she could not resist, and she smiled back. "No, I'm just living in the moment."

"I've been doing a lot of that myself."

"Good."

"I've been thinking, and you're right. Doris wouldn't want me to waste my life mourning over her. I need to rejoice for the time I had with her."

He smiled at Isabella. Lucas knew he would not tell her how he felt until she had placed her faith back where it belonged. Lucas owed her that time to find herself and identify with Christ as he had. He looked back into Isabella's chocolate eyes and commented, "God feels the same, in a way."

Lucas could tell he had gotten her attention. She raised her eyebrows and replied, "I don't want to talk about that, Lucas."

His heart broke for her. "All I'm saying is that God loves you."

"What do you want from me, Lucas?"

Frustrated that she could not confess all she was feeling, Lucas replied, "I'm at a loss, Isabella. I can't save you. As much as I want to take this hurt away from you, I can't."

Isabella brushed a piece of hair behind her ear. "What makes you think I need saving?"

"We all need saving."

Isabella waved her hands as though she did not want to hear another word. Lucas desired for her to desire Christ. Lucas closed his eyes and reminded himself that this was why he had to stay clear of her and let her heal alone.

Isabella took a breath. "Irene's expecting again. Did she tell you?"

Lucas smiled. "Yes. I heard from Shirley."

"You still talk with Shirley?"

Lucas knew that this would be a sore subject for Isabella if she reciprocated half of the love he felt for her. It was equally hard for him with Raymond. Isabella had to have known that. He nodded slowly. "Occasionally."

All he received was a head nod and a blank stare forward. Lucas knew that Isabella was stubborn and would not admit defeat easily. He would have to slowly drag her feelings out.

Chapter 17

New Orleans, 1933 (Five Years Later)

I sabella slipped on her brown evening dress, anticipating what the night had to offer. The year 1933 was a good year with the rising economy and the prohibition at an end. For Isabella though, it was exciting for another reason entirely. Tonight was her first large public outing since Doris passed. Although it had been five years now, the rumors and talk had not subsided. It was as if she was a fish in a tank of sharks waiting to devour her. Christmas was a time of joy and celebration, and Isabella wanted nothing more than that this year. The annual Christmas dance was always her favorite occasion during the season, but this night felt different. As Isabella powdered her face, she tried to exact her true concerns. Yes, Lucas would be there, but their friendship was mended for the most part. Irene, Fred, and Margaret would all attend, which should have been comforting to her. Isabella had a feeling that this dance would be different than the ones in the past. She rolled her eyes at herself in the mirror for thinking such idiotic things and dabbed her lips with red lipstick. Purse in hand, she walked into the living area to see Irene and her family ready to leave. Feeling as if she was holding them back, Isabella asked, "I'm so sorry. Am I running us late?"

"Not at all," Irene replied with a warm and friendly smile.

They packed into the automobile and made their way toward what used to be Raymond Dailey's father's mansion. Since Raymond was in prison and his father had passed, an uncle now owned the extravagant home. Isabella looked at the large walls and grandeur decorations as they pulled up to the home. Irene leaned over and commented, "Are you sure you don't want to fight for it?"

Isabella looked at the stunning home and then back to her friend. She wanted nothing to do with the Dailey family, and she sure did not want to own a home that large. In fact, it was already hard enough to purchase a small place of her own. She did not want to inconvenience her friends forever. Isabella replied, "I'll find a way to survive without the help of his family."

Irene smiled back at Isabella, which was a clear indication that she agreed. Isabella had always treasured that about her and Irene's friendship. Fred paid a man to park the car and the six of them entered the home. The massive Christmas tree met them in the entryway, and Isabella could tell Margaret was mesmerized by its size. Isabella took her hand and motioned to Irene, signaling that she could watch the child. Margaret pointed to Isabella's left and gave an excited yelp. She let go of Isabella and ran toward her object of affection. Isabella turned to see Lucas Matthews picking up his niece and spinning her around as if she weighed no more than a feather. It warmed her heart in more than one way. She was glad to see Margaret so happy, but on the other hand, she was pleased to see Lucas again. Isabella walked toward her old friend. "Merry Christmas, Lucas."

With a smile on his lips and a bounce in his step, Lucas replied, "Merry Christmas, Isabella."

Margaret tried to get her uncle's attention. "And Merry Christmas to my favorite niece, Ms. Margaret!"

Isabella gave him a smile as he motioned to Irene to take control of her child. Isabella was glad that Lucas wanted to talk with her alone, but was also plagued with intimidation. Maybe that was the reason she was so apprehensive. It was not Lucas, but the things he talked about that frightened her. She was now beginning to understand his concerns those five years ago. Isabella was grateful to Lucas for his harsh words then, because they had shaped her into the woman she was today.

"How are you?" he began as they walked around the grand tree.

"Well. And yourself?"

"Well."

The pause in the conversation began to drag a little until Lucas confessed, "I'm sorry, Isabella."

Isabella was confused as to why he was apologizing. "For?"

"Being absent these years. I thought you needed space and after that Thanksgiving I just…"

"There's no need to."

"I pushed you. I had no right to during that time in your life."

"No, Lucas, I needed that. I needed you." Isabella realized how romantic her confession sounded and added, "I needed you to show me that there was more to life than what I lost. I'm trying to see it. I guess I may never. That's the beauty in how it works."

Lucas looked at Isabella with tenderness, tenderness Isabella had not seen since their youth. Lucas took her hand and held it in his, then placed it on his heart. "Do you feel this?"

Isabella nodded, wondering what her friend was doing. Lucas let go of her hand and pointed to her heart, suggesting she put her hand on her chest. She gave him a curious look as she complied. Isabella giggled. "A heartbeat."

"Yes," Lucas stated. Isabella was completely confused.

"A heartbeat. Life. We have it because we live, but there's another kind of life, as you know, and I think Doris helped you find it."

Isabella looked at her friend and tried to comprehend what he was saying, but could not fathom where he was going with this tale and why he was telling it on Christmas Eve, of all nights.

He went on, "All her life, all you wanted was to protect Doris. Save her. In turn, Doris was protecting you. Doris was placed in your life to show you that you can't save yourself, no matter how much you want to, because only He has the power to save a life." It was as if Lucas was coming to the realization as the words rolled off his tongue. "That *was* the plan. That *is* the plan."

Isabella wiped the tears from her chocolate eyes and looked at her friend. Lucas was grinning up with compassion for their Creator. That second, she felt a weight lifted, and her anger was diminished. "I never thought of it that way."

Isabella looked at the ground and swallowed. Her eyes met Lucas's as she whispered, "She saved me."

Lucas was smiling with her, which Isabella found endearing. She looked at her friend, the man she thought she could never love, and finally let herself feel the love she had felt for him since the moment they met. Isabella was free. She looked at Lucas and commented, "I think they're about to sing."

"Yes, I believe so," he said as he led her into the main ballroom.

The crowd was large, and the scene was beautiful, but most importantly Isabella no longer felt resentment. She looked at Irene and her family, and knew that in that moment all was right. The conductor of the band led the crowd in the traditional medley they sang each year before the party began. As the lyrics resonated through the crowd, Isabella took a breath, taking a photograph with her mind. This was a memory to treasure.

The band was playing Christmas music on their brass instruments as Isabella walked up to Lucas and Irene. She smiled at her friend and stated, "It's a beautiful night."

"It is, isn't it?" Irene replied as she raised her glass of water.

Isabella got a blank stare from Lucas. It was like his eyes were peering into her every thought. She gave a small smile, but Lucas kept his eyes focused on hers. The music faded into a soft piano ballad, but Isabella's heart beat with a faster tempo. Lucas took her hand and asked politely, "Care to dance?"

Isabella looked at Irene and then back to Lucas. "Sure."

"I never thought you'd be where you are today," Lucas replied with a small upturn of the sides of his mouth.

Isabella did not know what to say to Lucas. It had been years since they had last connected as more than friends. She had a feeling that the romantic aspect of their relationship was coming out of its hibernation. The music was soft and so were the small glances Lucas stole as they twirled around the dance floor. Isabella was in a perfect dream, but concealed her giddy emotions carefully so that Lucas could not see. As the dance finished, the two friends thanked each other. Their attention was broken when a seven-year-old Margaret came running toward them.

"Uncle Lucas," the little girl said, "Did you see me dancing?"

Isabella's heart warmed as Lucas took the girl by the hand and turned her once. He replied, "Of course, my dear. How magnificent you are!"

"I told baby Marcus to dance with me."

"Baby Marcus is too young to dance, Margaret," Lucas replied with a kind touch to his niece's cheek.

Margaret looked so dismayed that Isabella offered up the best solution she knew possible. She knelt down to Margaret's level and suggested, "How about Uncle Lucas dances with you?"

Lucas smiled at Isabella, which gave her unexpected chills. "Good idea, Isabella. May I have this dance, Margaret?"

Margaret seemed enchanted that a man would ask her to dance. She was in awe of her young uncle, and Isabella was surely in awe of the man Lucas had become. She left the two alone on the dance floor and joined Irene at their table.

"Still not interested?" Irene asked as she raised one eyebrow, an expression Isabella feared came with an analysis of her behavior. Isabella looked at her friend and gave a small playful smile as she stated, "I don't know what you speak of."

Irene looked marvelous in her green dress, not much at all like she was expecting a third time. Isabella looked around for the little man and asked, "Where's Marcus?"

"With Fred, but that's not what we're talking about, is it?"

"What more do you want from me, Irene?"

"I want to know if my speculations are still true."

Isabella leaned closer to her friend and asked, "What speculations? It has been twenty-three years since I first thought I loved your brother. We were so young. It was 1910, for goodness' sake. So much has changed."

"You love him, Isabella, don't fool yourself into thinking otherwise."

Isabella was shocked that her friend would bring that subject up at a formal event, but Irene was clever. Isabella would have to give a calm answer. She looked at Irene with pleading eyes. "I know not…"

"You do, Isabella Archer."

Irene's look was cold and pierced through all Isabella's fears. Isabella scratched the back of her neck and replied slowly and quietly. "I do."

"Then it's true? You finally proudly admit it after all these years?"

Isabella looked at Lucas in his formal suit as he held and danced with a niece he treated like a daughter. She smiled. "I love him."

Irene laughed with what looked like significant relief. She placed her hand on her stomach and the other on Isabella's shoulder. "I'm glad you finally confessed it."

"How long have you suspected? I know a few years ago I confessed it, but I was depressed and…" Isabella asked her overjoyed friend.

"Since the day you two met. I knew. So it's not really new news to me. I've known for twenty-three years."

These words cut Isabella deep. Had she always loved Lucas and tried to conceal it or did she stop loving Lucas for a time? Either way, she robbed herself and Lucas of a life together. Isabella stared at the tablecloth as these questions stirred in her mind.

The dance finished, and Lucas made his way back to their table with Margaret. Isabella's guilt began to bubble. Lucas sat down at the table next to Isabella. She rose saying, "Excuse me." Lucas would ask where she was going, and Irene would come after her, but she did not care.

Isabella made it to the stairs. Footsteps were following her. Isabella hurried her pace and headed upward, not knowing the only place to go was onto the balcony of the home. As she reached the balcony, she closed the doors behind her, thankful to be the only one outside. The lights in the trees on the balcony reminded her that it was Christmas. Christmas was a time of celebration, not of sorrow and guilt. She sat on the cold bench and tried to make herself unseen. The door clicked behind her, and she knew Irene had found her. There was no way out of talking about it now. She closed her eyes and confessed, "I don't want to talk about him, Irene. It was so long ago. I said it three years ago, and I'm saying it again. There's no use in talking about it now."

"It's me, Lucas."

Isabella froze like the ice under her feet. She turned back and saw the man she loved. His dark suit and kind eyes mocked her as she sat on her throne of dismay. She stood and replied, "I thought you were Irene."

Lucas's mouth softly smiled. "It would appear so."

He walked toward her, but she stood still, paralyzed. "I don't know what you think I was…"

The tenderness Isabella saw in Lucas's eyes was an amount she had never seen before. "But I think I do."

Lucas's heart pounded so loud he was sure Isabella heard its every beat. This was the moment he had waited for, and he had to make the best of it. He approached her with care, knowing that she would close off at any moment. "Isabella, what did you tell my sister?"

He could sense her nervous behavior and wished she knew just how nervous he was feeling. He came face to face with Isabella and asked, "What's eating you?"

"What happened after my parents' accident? Why did you suggest we stay only friends?"

"You were going through so much. I thought you wanted time."

"If I wanted time I would've asked for it," Isabella replied with blurry eyes.

Lucas looked at the woman he loved, and in a moment of confidence, took her hands in his. "I loved you, Isabella."

Isabella seemed surprised by his sudden clasp. "You did?"

Lucas's heart broke. He shamed himself for not telling her that day. "I most certainly did."

Isabella moved slightly closer to him. "I did too."

Lucas's heart swelled. "I always have."

"Truly?" Isabella asked as if she already knew the answer to the question.

Lucas put his hand under her jaw. "I love you."

"I love you too."

As the answer rolled off her tongue, Lucas pulled her close and kissed her lips. It was a quiet moment where life stopped and time itself was replaced with a simple expression of love in its truest form; a simple kiss to seal a lifetime of love finally revealed through words.

Isabella pulled away from the kiss with a smile. "I thought you'd never tell me."

"I thought you never felt it."

Isabella tucked a piece of her hair behind her ear and asked, "So what does this mean?"

"I assume you'll take my offer and carry out the rest of this night as a proper date, and then tomorrow we'll go from there."

"I'd like that very much," she said with an incandescent smile. Her heart fluttered as he offered his arm. Isabella put her arm through his. She could feel his pulse through his sleeve. She let out a small laugh. "Your heart is as loud as a stampede of elephants."

Lucas rolled his eyes, and Isabella could not help but let out another laugh. She saw their reflection in the windowed doors. This was the moment she had thought about since she first saw Lucas Matthews, and it was finally here. In a moment, Isabella realized that every horrid thing that had occurred since their first meeting was all leading to this moment. They walked down the stairs and were greeted by a very happy and very pregnant Irene. She threw her arms around Isabella and whispered in her ear, "I told you."

As she pulled away, Irene repeated, "I told you both."

Isabella saw the joyful tears in her friend's eyes. Even through all the late nights and frightful dreams, Irene was there telling Isabella that all would right itself in the end. She saw the bigger picture. Fred came up behind his wife and commented, "She's been waiting a long time for this. We both have."

Lucas looked at his sister with small eyes. "What are you crying about?"

Lucas was only teasing his sister, but she blushed anyway.

Later, Marcus and Margaret joined the rest of the family for supper, but Lucas could not keep his eyes off Isabella. He knew he loved her, he had known for a long time. Maybe it was the way she looked, or maybe it was the way he felt to have finally confessed his suppressed feelings, but Lucas had never felt so alive. When he looked at Isabella from the side, he saw the profile of his future wife. He had always seen her in this light, but to know she loved him back was enough motivation to propose right there. Yet he knew he must make the engagement spectacular and memorable. Lucas had waited for so long, so, it had to be perfect. He ate a piece of ham and smiled as Isabella's eyes met his. He took his hand off the table and reached for hers. She gave him a kind smile, which made him all the more grateful that he had waited for her.

The night drew to a close, and the other members of Lucas's family had to depart early to lay the children down for the night. Isabella leaned over to Lucas. "I'll see you tomorrow morning."

"Are you not staying with me for a while?" he asked, hoping he and Isabella could talk and decide exactly what they were to one another.

Isabella flashed a small grin and replied, "I think it best I ride back with Irene and help her put the children down."

Lucas felt a slight pull on his heart. "Very well. I'll see you tomorrow."

He helped Isabella into the car and waved good-bye as the whole family drove away into the black night.

That night, Isabella burst through Irene's door saying, "Irene, I told Lucas I love him. I actually did it!"

At this sentence, Fred gave his wife and her friend an understanding nod as he excused himself, "I think I'll take another bath."

Isabella waited until Fred had exited the room before she jumped on Irene's bed like a young girl. She smiled and then laughed into a pillow. After her excess excitement was gone, Isabella turned to her friend and asked, "What do I do?"

"Nothing," Irene blankly replied as she fixed a curler on her head.

"I have to do something."

"He's the man. Let him be the man."

Isabella's eyes grew wide as the thought of marriage crossed her mind. "Will he propose?"

Irene gave her friend an annoyed look. "I don't know."

"You're his sister, you must know. You know everything," Isabella pleaded with her hands crossed.

"Trust in His timing, Isabella," Irene reminded a headstrong and love-struck Isabella.

Isabella nodded in agreement and then gave her friend another girlish giggle. She threw a pillow at Irene and replied in a playful manner, "I hope it's sooner rather than later."

"Don't we all," her friend joked as Isabella left the room for her bedroom.

Chapter 18

Lucas woke up at five o'clock the next morning to clean every inch of his home. He started with the kitchen and worked his way into the living room. He wrapped a large stuffed bear Margaret had eyed in the toy store. He decided to store it in his room, because little Margaret was a mischievous one and would guess it the first time she laid eyes on it.

He began to cook the ham, one of the only things he was capable of cooking alone. Lucas was grateful that Isabella and Irene had agreed to come early and help with the side dishes. His heart jumped when Isabella entered into his mind, but he continued to prep the ham so that it was ready when the rest of his family arrived.

Lucas turned his attention to the living area where the majority of the day would be spent. He could not wait for the opening of presents that lay under the Christmas tree.

He had one thing for each of his family members, but felt bad that the only thing he had for the woman he loved was a pair of socks. Lucas wandered into his room and looked for the engagement ring he had kept for Isabella in his side table drawer. He gently opened the box it came in. Lucas smiled when he saw its simple glow. He tried to imagine it on Isabella's hand, but he had no image come to mind. Lucas should propose to her, he thought, but was it too soon? A journal caught his eye, and Lucas decided to write down whether or not he should propose to Isabella. He wanted this moment to be etched in time. Lucas flipped to the last page of the journal and bled through his pen. He placed the ring on the table beside his bed, not really sure what to do with it or how he would even bring up the subject. He stashed Marcus's toy on a shelf for safekeeping. Just as he did this, company arrived.

The doorbell rang, and Fred entered with Marcus and Margaret. Lucas came out of his room in a hurry and closed the door to hide the children from their toys. Lucas was pleased to see Fred and his niece and nephew. "Uncle Lucas!" the children cried as they ran into his arms.

"My, my, how you've grown."

Margaret tossed her brown curls over her shoulder. "You just saw us last night!"

Their father entered into the conversation and said, "You're just getting so big. Uncle Lucas is as surprised as I am."

"I did help Mama and Aunt Isabella with the green beans," she stated with her hands on her hips.

"You did? Well, I can't wait to have some of your special green beans," Lucas said as the door opened behind him.

"There they are!"

Lucas turned to see Isabella with a pot and a basket in her hands. He stood and took the basket off the pot so she could see. Her eyes met his. "I hear our green beans were made by a special girl."

Isabella smiled. "That's right. Margaret's a great cook."

The grin on Margaret's face brought laughter to them both. He looked at Isabella and stated, "You look very nice today."

"Thank you," she replied as she made her way into the kitchen.

Lucas followed her. "Did you sleep?"

"No."

"Same." Lucas watched as Isabella began to peel the potatoes he had purchased the day before. He took one. "Let me help."

Isabella gave him a strange look, questioning why he was helping her in the kitchen. He smiled at her and tried to conceal the secret question that he was dying to ask her. He finished one potato and asked, "Can we talk?"

"We're talking now," Isabella said with a smile on her face.

Lucas shook his head. "I meant alone."

Isabella looked behind her shoulder. "We are alone."

Lucas picked up another potato and asked, "So what are we doing exactly?"

"Making mashed potatoes."

"You know what I mean."

Isabella placed her potato in the peeled pile, and looked at Lucas with squinted eyes. "What do you want us to be?"

Lucas thought for a moment. "I'd like you to be my girl."

"Okay, I guess that means we're together."

"Now you're on the trolley!" Lucas exclaimed a little too loud.

Irene yelled back to her brother, "Pipe down in there."

Lucas and Isabella looked at each other and laughed as they finished the remainder of the potatoes.

"I believe it's time to open presents!" Isabella exclaimed.

Margaret's face lit up like the lights on the Christmas tree. She reached for the closest present with her name on it and began to open the gift. Margaret got a new doll, two new dresses, and a new pair of shoes. Marcus got a toy train and new clothes. Irene's turn came, and she got a new pair of socks, a new pan, and a bracelet from her husband. Fred received a new watch, socks, and a briefcase. The time came for Isabella to open her gifts, but she was only excited about the man she was sitting beside. He handed her two gifts, a new pan and a new pair of shoes from Irene. Lucas's gift came last, and she was sure it would not be grand. She opened the box and took out a pair of socks that matched Irene's. Isabella smiled and looked at Lucas. He was blushing from ear to ear. She smiled and patted him on the leg to allude to the fact that she appreciated the gift. He opened his gifts quickly. Lucas received a new briefcase and a shirt. Isabella was nervous when he opened her journal. She was relieved when he flipped through its pages and thanked her with a small kiss on the top of her head. The children played by the fire until dinner was served. The meal was scrumptious, and the company was delightful, an ideal Christmas for Isabella.

"I think hot cocoa is in order," Lucas declared as the family made their way to the furnace.

Isabella helped him carry in the hot drinks and fluffy marshmallows that accented the tops of their cocoa. As they were all settling down, Lucas shot up once again and asked Isabella to follow him into his bedroom. Isabella was reluctant to follow him, but when he mentioned he had a surprise for Margaret and Marcus, Isabella knew it meant another toy for each of the children. She knew Lucas too well to guess otherwise. She followed Lucas into his room and asked, "What did you get them?"

"A stuffed bear and a toy car. I thought I'd save the best for last."

Isabella walked toward Lucas to help with the large animal, but as she did, she lost her balance on the leftover wrapping paper. Isabella fell into the side table with a *thud*. Lucas sat the car on his bed and came to her side. When Isabella's embarrassment wore off, she began to laugh at herself. "That was quite clever."

Lucas's laugh softened her bruised ego. "Let's get back in there."

Isabella's backside was particularly uncomfortable, so she reached under herself to see what she was sitting on. It felt odd and rectangular, maybe one of Marcus's blocks. She pulled the object out from under her and examined it. Her heart stopped when she realized what was inside the small box. She passed it to Lucas, who was sitting beside her with shaking hands. "I think this is yours."

She saw pure joy in his eyes that could outshine any star. Lucas took her hand and helped her to her feet. He drew her close and confessed, "You found me out too soon."

Lucas motioned for her to sit on the bed, and out of sheer shock and elation, Isabella complied.

Lucas looked at the box and then to Isabella. This day had always seemed like a distant future, but in that slight fraction of a second everything had fallen perfectly into place. Lucas tucked a piece of Isabella's dark hair behind her ear and gave her the picture of them he could no longer conceal. She laughed at their young faces long enough to distract her from Lucas's shaking voice.

He took a knee and held Isabella's hand. "I've never not loved you, Isabella. From the day I met you I knew you would one day be my wife." Lucas paused to wipe away the happy tears that fell on Isabella's face. "I love you with everything that I am and everything I have. You are my light, you are my love, and you give me life. Not just any life, but a life to live to the fullest, and I promise to love you every day of it. I always have. I always will. Isabella Marie Archer, will you be my wife?"

Lucas waited in silence for a teary eyed Isabella to comprehend the question, and for a moment, he feared she might run from her feelings. Then, in a second, his lips were pressed on hers after a faint whisper of a "yes."

After a moment, Lucas pulled away. "We have presents to deliver."

Isabella tried to clear her face of her happy tears. "We do."

Lucas slipped the ring on her finger where it had always belonged.

As the two came into the room with the presents, the little ones were quick to open them. Irene turned to Isabella and saw the tearstains in her makeup. Isabella showed Irene the ring on her finger. When Fred and Irene pieced together the message, they both stood and congratulated the couple. The newly engaged Lucas and Isabella played with the children and their presents. The sun went down, and the moon rose as Fred sat to play the piano. The Matthews gathered around him and sang as well as they could. This Christmas they had many reasons to celebrate. Isabella placed her head on Lucas's shoulder as they all sang "Hark! The Herald Angels Sing." Isabella looked around the room at the many radiant faces and was thankful that she now experienced that same joy. Margaret sang loudly and a bit off-key, and Marcus mumbled their Christmas favorite. Isabella closed her eyes and thought of Doris, her precious baby girl. She opened her eyes to see Lucas staring back. Sweet tears fell from her cheeks as she listened to the melodious and triumphant lyrics of the classic Christmas hymn.

"Hail the heaven-born Prince of Peace!
Hail the Son of Righteousness!
Light and life to all he brings,
Risen with healing in his wings.
Mild he lays his glory by,
Born that we no more may die,
Born to raise the sons of earth,
Born to give them second birth.
Hark! The herald angels sing,
"Glory to the new born King!"

(Charles Wesley, 1739)

Epilogue

I sabella lived fifty more years, and each day was spent with Lucas. She watched her two sons grow and marry women who were much like her. She saw three of her grandchildren born. Raymond may have taken Doris from her, but Doris lived on through Isabella. As for Raymond, he was never seen again, locked away, forgotten, but forgiven. Ms. Isabella Archer-Dailey lived a happy childhood, but a grave adult life. On the contrary, Mrs. Isabella Matthews lived a life full of love, forgiveness, and redemption. Lucas was more than a love to Isabella; he was a friend, a guide, and a reminder that God makes beautiful things out of terrible circumstances.

I found my husband's diary among his things when he passed. When I look back on the life I led, I see that Christ is the one who inspired it all. Now, I reside in the love of my children and grandchildren, while my Lucas resides with baby

Doris. May 13, 1975, Lucas passed on, leaving our children and me behind.

I loved him, yes, and I still do. In the last entry he wrote in his first diary, he said that I was someone worth writing about, but I disagree. Lucas Matthews was a rare man. A man who stayed by my side through every trial I faced. Men like Lucas are hard to come across, and I was a lucky lady to have him. I fought him for so long, and I see now that was a mistake.

You see, love is a strange thing; you can go your whole life searching for it, but never really understand what it is until it is staring you in the face. Then, once it's gone, it's gone, and no one has yet to figure out how to get it back. The thing with love is that you can't be afraid to take it when it comes, because you never know when it will come again or how long it will last. Well, my love for Lucas will never fade, and that is something worth writing about. *He* is something worth writing about.

CPSIA information can be obtained at www.ICGtesting.com
Printed in the USA
LVOW10s1559240516

489736LV00021B/535/P